Guide to the Museum
of Decorative Arts, Paris

This guide was written by Jérôme Coignard in close
collaboration with the museum's curators.

Les Arts Décoratifs

Hélène David-Weill, president

Sophie Durrleman, general director

Béatrice Salmon, museums director

Renata Cortinovis, development director

Monique Blanc,
curator, Middle Ages-Renaissance

Chantal Bouchon,
curator, Prints and Drawings

Dorothée Charles,
curator, Toys

Dominique Forest,
curator, Modern-Contemporary, Jewellery

Véronique de La Hougue,
curator, Wallpaper

Odile Nouvel-Kammerer,
curator, 19th Century

Jean-Luc Olivié,
curator, Glass

Evelyne Possémé,
curator, Art Nouveau-Art Deco, Jewellery

Bertrand Rondot,
curator, 17th-18th Century

Acknowledgements
Jérôme Coignard wishes to thank the curators of the Musée
des Arts Décoratifs and Jean-Luc Larribau for their invaluable
contribution to this guide.

Translated from the French
David Wharry

Editorial coordination
Chloé Demey, assisted by Halima Millet

Graphic design and layout
CL Design

Proof reading
Halima Millet

Guide to the Museum of Decorative Arts, Paris

SilvanaEditoriale

Words with an asterisk * are explained in the glossary at the end of the guide.
The ◉ sign indicates the work is reproduced.
The black disks ⓱ indicate room numbers.
The red disks ❸ indicate levels in the museum space.

Contents

Preface

Les Arts Décoratifs takes you on a fascinating and moving journey through the centuries, from the Middle Ages to the present day.

This journey was made possible by a group of industrialists, collectors and craftsmen who joined forces in the late 19th century to 'nurture in France the culture of the arts which pursue the realisation of the beautiful in the useful'.

Many of them bequeathed objects they cherished and lived with to the museum, and this is what gives our museum its very special, 'domestic' feeling. The pledge of its founders has been upheld to this day. Roaming through each room, you will find yourself at the very heart of the aspirations of all those who have sought to make our lives easier, happier and more beautiful.

In the rooms and period rooms, showcases of taste and craftsmanship, in the study spaces focussing on the evolution of furniture, materials and objects with specific uses, or immersing yourself in the world of toys, another story will unfold, the history of the constant necessity for imagination, perfection and dreams.

Hélène David-Weill

Forward

The first guide to the Musée des Arts Décoratifs, *Guide sommaire, à travers le musée des Arts décoratifs,* was published when the museum opened in the Marsan pavilion of the Louvre in 1905. It was reprinted three times, in 1906, 1908 and 1909. Its succinct, unillustrated descriptions of the rooms, then on levels 2 and 3, were accompanied only by a few plans. The text on the history of the museum and its statutes recalled its singular status as an institution: the fruit of private initiative and a non-profit-making organisation approved by the state since 1882, in exchange for the allocation of its premises by the state, it had to furnish them at its own expense. Furthermore, despite receiving no public funding and being obliged to spend the entire proceeds from admission fees on the upkeep and enrichment of its collections, after 15 years those collections were to become state property.

The next guide, illustrated this time, was not published until 1926.

A new revised and enlarged edition was published in 1934. In its opening pages, as before, it recalled the aims that had led to the institution's founding, but this time with a significant addition. 'By virtue of the law of 24 August 1920 renewing the convention with the State, the museum staff is now remunerated by means of a subsidy from the State, to whom all the works belong, but *the enrichment, installation and upkeep of these collections are to be financed solely by the Union Centrale des Arts Décoratifs.* Admission fees and members' subscriptions will therefore be contributing to the life and prosperity of a national institute for the education of the applied arts'.

These same principles still apply today, exactly a century after the museum first opened. In 2006, entirely refurbished after its ten-year closure and the signing of a new convention with the state, it has opened its doors to the public once more. For the first time, in 9,000m² of redesigned exhibition spaces, a selection of some 6,000 objects from all periods will provide a new insight into the decorative arts and their diverse techniques.

This new guide will accompany you through the collections chronologically, from the Middle Ages to the present day, drawing your attention to their many facets and helping you to appreciate them. In parallel and to enrich your journey through the centuries, punctuated by the period rooms, the guide focuses on aspects of contemporary life, techniques and the great personalities that have marked this comprehensive history of the decorative arts.

You will also be introduced to the thematic departments: the graphic arts, jewellery, toys, wallpaper and glass. Displayed in specific exhibition spaces or mingling with other artistic fields in the chronological presentations, they contribute fully to the rich fabric of the museum.

Many of these displays will be regularly renewed, particularly those in the Study Galleries, the Toy Gallery and the Dubuffet Gallery. Displaying works on a rotary basis is necessary for conservation reasons but also to encourage our public to return often to discover more.

We wish you a very pleasant visit.

Béatrice Salmon

Middle Ages

The reign of Saint Louis in the 12th century was a fertile and innovative period in western art. The Gothic style began to establish itself around 1140 at the instigation of Abbot Suger in the abbey church and royal necropolis at Saint Denis. Gradually demarcating itself from the Romanesque style out of which it developed, Gothic art reached its peak between around 1190 and 1260. The decorative motifs of the Gothic cathedrals, with their tracery and rosette windows, also pervaded the decorative arts.

In his innovative first novel, *Erec and Enide* (1165), Chrétien de Troyes (c.1135–85) focussed on the destiny of its hero rather than merely chronicling a narrative. *The Romance of the Rose* (1230–70), begun by Guillaume de Lorris and finished by Jean de Meung, is the great masterpiece of Medieval literature.

Another tradition which emerged in the 12th century was the international fair. The counts of Champagne organised fairs on an unprecedented scale, to which people flocked from Italy, Germany and the Near East to sell woollen cloth, silks, garments and other finery. Merchants and craftsmen organised themselves into guilds. In craftsmen's workshops and at the universities, especially the Sorbonne, practical and theoretical knowledge circulated increasingly freely.

1328 marked the end of the Capetian dynasty and the beginning of the Hundred Years War, during the reign of Philippe VI of Valois. The political crises from 1340 onwards were compounded by the terrible plague of 1348, which wiped out half the population. Despite devastating incursions by the English, the arts and letters flourished in France during the reigns of Charles V and Charles VI. In the late 15th century, Louis XI unified the kingdom and laid the first foundations of modern France. The Italian Wars that began in 1491, although disastrous militarily, brought the new transalpine art back to France and sowed the seeds of the French Renaissance.

De 1364 à 1380
Reign of Charles V the Wise.
Courtly art reaches its peak.

De 1328 à 1440
The Hundred Years War.

1453
Fall of the Byzantine Empire.

1491
Charles VIII's marriage to Anne, Duchess of Brittany, unifies the last independent kingdom with France. Beginning of the Italian Wars.

Millefleur tapestry
(detail, see p. 27)

Middle Ages

The three artistic movements running through the first rooms are: the Early Gothic age, during which the great cathedrals at Chartres, Amiens and Reims were built and Marian worship developed, then the 'courtly' and International Gothic styles which developed at court and at the residences of the great patrons, and finally Late Gothic, a transitional period in which Italian elements began to mingle with Gothic decorative motifs.

The Bible in pictures

Two famous collections amassed in the late 19th and early 20th century by Emile Peyre and Jules Maciet graced the museum with an exceptional collection of European altarpieces dating from the Middle Ages to the Renaissance.

An altarpiece—the French word, *retable,* is derived from the Latin *retro tabula* and the ancient French *rere* ('behind') and *table* ('plank')—is a decorated panel placed on an altar. Altarpieces, in painted wood, stone, metal, marble or alabaster, played a key role in liturgy. Their sumptuous depictions of scenes from the Bible were intended to both dazzle and edify the congregation.

The Altarpiece Gallery ❶, evoking the nave of a church, is separated from the forenave by screens from the Château de Villeneuve-Lembron in Auvergne. The Lombard sculptor Giovanni Buora's stone figure of the *Virgin* 👁 (c.1480) is strikingly humble and dignified. The base with palm leaves and flowers fitted into a funerary monument.

The *Figure of a Prophet* 👁, attributed to the Lombard sculptor Pietro Bussolo and dating from the 1490s, is perhaps Isaac. Sculpted in limewood, a soft wood frequently used by sculptors, it was painted, gilded* and silvered. The very expressive modelling of the face, prominent veins on the hands and graceful drapery are the hallmarks of a great artist. Altarpieces were frequently sculpted with in-the-round* figures like this, which was removed from the original work in a church in Bergamo. The Latin inscription on the unscrolled phylactery*—*Ego sum pater tuus noli timere no morieris*— seems to refer to a verse in Genesis (XXVI, 24): 'I am the God of your father Abraham. Do not be afraid, for I am with you'.

The struggle between Good and Evil

Saint George Slaying the Dragon 👁 is attributed to the artist known as the Master of Rabenden, active in Bavaria c.1510–25. The ineffable gentleness of his face contrasts with the stiffness of his armour, largely concealed by his tunic, whose swirling lower right drapery reoccurs like a signature in other works by the same sculptor. The worship of the soldier martyr George was very popular among the Greeks of Constantinople and practiced in the Holy Roman Empire from the reign of Emperor Henry II (died 1024), who consecrated a church in his name at Bamberg. But it was above all during the era of the crusaders, who adopted George as their patron saint, that depictions of the saint on horseback slaying the dragon, symbolising the triumph of good over evil, became widespread in Europe.

The 'Virgin Mary'
Giovanni Buora
Stone, traces of polychromy
Venice, early 16th century

'Saint George Slaying the Dragon'
Attributed to the Master of Rabenden
Polychromed limewood
Upper Bavaria, c.1515–20

'Figure of a Prophet'
Pietro Bussolo
Polychromed limewood
Lombardy, c.1490

13

The art of the sculptor

Several display cases in the Altarpiece Gallery contain parts of altarpieces from Italy, France and Northern Europe. Although separated from the original work, these fragments can be appreciated as works in their own right. Some are the equal of the carved stone figures decorating the portals of the greatest cathedrals of Europe. The angels, magi and saints by German masters, some of whose masterpieces were sculpted during the flamboyant 'swansong' of the Late Gothic Period, are dominated by the exquisitely naive painted and gilded* Virgin, sculpted in Franconia around 1500. With her hands joined in prayer and a smile on her realistically portrayed, still juvenile face, she is looking slightly to the left, towards the annunciating Angel Gabriel, who has since disappeared. Her long undulating hair contrasts with the angular folds of her mantle.

Attributed to the workshop of Paul Lautensack, active in Bamberg from 1501 to 1528, *Visitation* ● was part of the wing of an altarpiece. The meeting of the two pregnant women, the Virgin Mary and her cousin Elisabeth, mother of Saint John the Baptist, is depicted with tenderness and a sense of wonder, as if the two holy women were already aware of the destinies of their offspring. The drapery falling from their touching stomachs mingles in an extremely elegant composition. The youthful plumpness of the Virgin Mary, draped in gold, contrasts with the more slender figure of her already elderly cousin.

'Visitation'
Workshop of Paul Lautensack
Polychromed limewood
Bamberg, c.1510–15

The crafts of the altarpiece

The creation of an altarpiece was a collective enterprise. The joiner, sculptor, gilder and painter would often work for a single master, who received the commission, conceived the work, allocated tasks and supervised their execution. In the late Middle Ages, written contracts became widespread. They stipulated the date by which the work had to be finished, terms of payment, the materials to be used and often the client's wishes concerning the depiction of the subject.

The joiner made the coffer and sometimes the decorative elements, the sculptor sculpted the statuettes and relief figures on the panels, often also polychroming them, and the gilder applied the gold leaf on the brown, red or orange-coloured undercoat painted on the wood, then browned or polished it with a hard stone. Altarpieces usually had painted wings that were opened only during religious festivals. The painter had to carefully prepare each panel before painting it, filling in knots and imperfections then sticking a thin canvas to it before applying several coats of chalk or plaster-based primer. The tempera technique, which consisted in mixing pigments with glue, egg or milk, was gradually superseded by oil paint in the 15th century.

'Altarpiece of the Passion of Christ'
Master of the View of Saint Gudule
Coffer: sculpted, painted and gilded oak;
wings: oil on wood
Brussels, c.1490

**'Polyptych of the Virgin and Child
Surrounded by Saints'**
Antonio De Carro
Tempera on wood, gilt ground
Emilia, dated 1398

International Gothic

The monumental *Polyptych of the Virgin and Child Surrounded by Saints* ● (p. 16-17) by the Piacenza-born artist Antonio De Carro (c.1360–c.1421), has an invaluable inscription on the predella* ❷.

It includes the name of the monk who commissioned it, Lucas De Coddis de Marano, the date, 1398, and the name of the artist, 'Ant. De Cairo'. It is the only painting signed by this artist, who was still unknown twenty years ago. Antonio De Carro was the most important painter of the Trecento in Piacenza and one of the most endearing figures of International Gothic, the elegant style which bloomed throughout Europe in the 14th century. The donor is portrayed in prayer at the Virgin's feet. The panels with gilt grounds are set in a rigorously composed replica of a Gothic church, with pillars, arches, pinnacles* and gables*. Only a few of this altarpiece's lateral elements are missing, which is rare for a work removed from its original location long ago.

Another of the collection's masterpieces is the altarpiece in the International Gothic style by Luis Borrassá ● (c.1420), a Catalan artist active in Barcelona between 1380 and 1424. The centre panel shows Saint John the Baptist preaching in the desert, wearing a tunic lined with camel's skin. His staff is crowned by the Mystic Lamb, symbolising Christ's sacrifice on the Cross. The inscription on the phylactery* reads *'Ecce agnus Dei qui tollit pe[c]a...'* ('Here is the Lamb of God who removes sin'). Above, dominating the entire work, the Crucifixion, while the three scenes on either side tell the saint's story, from the announcement of his birth to his father, the prophet Zachariah, to his decapitation, ordered by Salome.

Similar sumptuous brocade costumes, vividly coloured fabrics and extravagant headdresses—the one worn by Herodias, for example—can be seen in the *Very Rich Hours of the Duke of Berry* by the Limbourg brothers. The attention Borassá paid to depicting ordinary everyday objects (in the birth scene, for example) ranks him among the great masters of the International Gothic style. The entire composition is painted with great finesse except for the predella, which may have been executed by one of his apprentices. The Christ of Pity in the middle is flanked by Saint Peter, Saint Andrew and the Virgin Mary on one side, and Saint John the Evangelist, Saint James and Saint Paul on the other.

The *imago pietatis* ('image of piety'), which originated in Italy in the late 13th century, conveys the vision Saint Gregory had while celebrating mass. This altarpiece still has its original, typically Spanish frame or *guardapolvo* ('protection against dust').

The indispensable chest

Altarpieces often reproduced the rib vaulting, arcatures, columns and pinnacles of the Gothic cathedrals in miniature, but lay furniture also used architectural decoration. In the 13th century, even kings and great lords still lived relatively modestly. Their furniture often consisted merely of a bed, a chest, a bench, a scabelle* and one or two trestle tables, as they often had to leave at short notice for political or economic reasons. The taste for pomp did not develop until the following century, during the reign of Philippe VI of Valois (1328–50). Luxury manifested itself initially in the sumptuousness of

Altarpiece of Saint John the Baptist and its predella
Luis Borrassá
Tempera on wood
Catalonia, c.1420

textile wall hangings, cushions, plaited mats, carpets and tapestries, which, with precious crockery and jewellery were the true barometers of munificence.

The medieval chest, which often had handles on the sides, was used for storing all kinds of objects, provisions, crockery, small pieces of furniture and wall hangings which, since life was not yet completely sedentary, had to be transported from one residence to another.

The oak *Chest with Trellis Armature* ◉ is a superb and rare example of this type of reinforcement, which can still be seen on church doors. The armature* here is more decorative than functional, however. Metal reinforcement disappeared in the next century, replaced by invisible assembly techniques such as wooden dowels. This chest is one of the most ancient pieces of furniture in a French museum. The doors of a sacristy cupboard from the Somme region illustrate the same construction principle. Its armatures, more intricate and originally entirely gilt*, are decorated with oak leaves on one side and ivy leaves on the other.

The chest, originally used merely for storage, underwent numerous metamorphoses: when given a back and armrests it became the cathedra, with doors on one side and raised on legs it became the dresser, and eventually, in the 17th century, the chest of drawers. And of course when it has a flat lid it can be used as bench, table or even a bed.

An enigmatic Florentine master

In the late 13th-century Florentine altarpiece attributed to the enigmatic Master of the Magdalene ◉, the hieratic figure of the Virgin and Child, enthroned between Saint Andrew and Saint James, takes up the whole height of the picture. The tiered scenes on either side are a typically Tuscan device. Reading from left to right and from top to bottom, they are: the Annunciation, the Nativity, the Adoration of the Magi, the Presentation in the Temple, the Flight into Egypt, and the Dormition of the Virgin. The engraved gold ground and the stylisation of the faces and drapery show the enduring influence of Byzantine canons or *maniera greca*. In the 1920s, an art historian named this anonymous artist after his picture depicting the life of Mary Magdalene, now in the Accademia in Florence. His prolific output and the many works attributed to his entourage suggest he must have employed a large number of artists in his workshop. *Virgin and Child* is regarded as his finest work.

Arranged around this priceless 'icon' are works in the International Gothic style. The iconography of the altarpiece panel with three scenes from the life of Christ ◉, formerly attributed to Luis Borrassá and now to Jaime and Pere Serra, also Catalan, is extremely original, particularly the Resurrection. The Serras added the Virgin praying in a window and a cypress tree, symbol of both death and permanence, to the traditional image of Christ rising from the Tomb while the two soldiers are sleeping. The presence of Virgin next to her resuscitated son is a hallmark of the painters of the Serras' entourage. This feature has been attributed to the possible influence of the

Nativity, Epiphany, Resurrection
The Serra workshop
Tempera on wood
Catalonia, c.1395

**Altarpiece of the Virgin and Child
with Saint Andrew and Saint James**
Master of the Magdalene
Tempera on wood, gold ground
Florence, c.1275–80

Chest with trellis armature
Oak, wrought iron
France, late 13th century

sermons of the famous preacher Saint Vincent Ferrier, known to have been in Barcelona between 1372 and 1376.

A blaze of red angels

One of the major works of the museum's Spanish collection, the *Coronation of the Virgin* ☉ (c.1480), by the Aragon-born painter Juan de la Abadia the Elder, is a fragment from the centre panel of an altarpiece. Its most distinctive features are the elegance of the figures, the original treatment of the angels and the intense spirituality it exudes. Christ, amidst a blaze of red angels, is crowning his kneeling mother, a composition perhaps derived from early 15th-century French illuminators.

A fragment of a panel attributed to Jan Van Eyck shows that architectural motifs were not used solely in sculpted frames but also pervaded painting. Depicted with a spidery delicateness worthy of an illuminator, this fragile edifice may have once crowned a Virgin and Child.

The legend of Saint Elpidius

These eight polyptych panels depicting *Scenes from the Life of Saint Elpidius,* were painted by Giacomo Di Nicola da Recanati, an artist known from 1433 to 1466. Framed with sculpted and gilt* oak arcatures and cabled columns, they recount the life of an evangelist saint venerated in the Marche region, who would have been portrayed, either painted or sculpted, in the missing central part. The artist set his elegantly and ornately dressed figures, typical of the International Gothic style, in a decorous landscape with architec-

ture, a palace, a castle, a portico and a prison. The polyptych was painted for the collegiate church of Sant'Elpidio a Mare, a small town in the Marche, near Fermo. In the first panel, Elpidius is visiting King Antony. Struck by the saint's radiant beauty, the king offered him his daughter's hand and half of his kingdom, on the condition that he renounced his faith... The Musée des Arts Décoratifs and the Petit Palais in Avignon are the only French museums to have works by Giacomo Di Nicola da Recanati.

There is the same naturalism in the sculpture of the period. In one of the display cases devoted to sculpture in wood, the *Virgin of the Nativity* ☉ (Île-de-France, c.1330–40) shows the effort 14th-century artists made to humanise Christ's mother. Sitting up in bed, she is supporting the Infant Jesus as he takes his first steps. A delightful detail of this altarpiece fragment is the heads of the ox and donkey above the empty, manger-like cradle. The display case of stone sculptures contains fragments of funerary architecture, while the alabaster tympanums ☉ (Catalonia, 14th century) shows Gothic already at its peak, but it would continue in Northern France and northern Europe for much longer.

'Coronation of the Virgin'
Juan de la Abadia the Elder
Tempera on wood
Aragon, c.1480

'Virgin of the Nativity'
Polychromed walnut, gold
Île-de-France, c.1330–40

Nativity
Alabaster, traces of polychromy
Catalonia, 14th century

The bedroom of a high-ranking dignitary

In the second half of the 15th century, interior decoration became increasingly sculptural, relegating textiles to a secondary role without eclipsing them entirely. Joiners decorated furniture with architectural elements—pinnacles*, arcatures and windows—and the linenfold motif appeared.

Most of the furniture in this bedroom ◉ ❸ came from the Château de Villeneuve-Lembron, the home of Rigault d'Oureille (1455–1517), Seneschal of Gascony, equerry to Louis XI, then butler to Charles VIII, Louis XII and François I. The linenfold decoration on the sides of the bed and the wall panelling was sculpted with a curved plane.

The long, thin bench for sitting by the fire and the cathedra are also sculpted with the same motif, which remained popular in France and Flanders until the early 16th century. The four-poster bed, Italian-influenced, appeared in France in the late 15th century. It was given pride of place in the bedroom, next to the fireplace. This one has columns supporting the canopy, which is sculpted with Rigault d'Oureille's coat-of-arms, and of course curtains to protect the sleeper from the cold.

The chair on the right of the bed was reserved for the lord and his lady. In the second half of the 15th century, the lower part concealed a chest. Like the divine throne of Christ and the Virgin Mary depicted in altarpieces, and like the royal throne, the chair was a symbol of power, in this case temporal. The room was lit by the fireplace, with its pyramidal hood, sculpted lintel, firedogs, cast-iron plaque and shovel, and also, when there were guests, by a bronze wall lamp and tallow or wax candles.

Bedroom of Rigault d'Oureille
Coffer bench
Four-poster bed

Dresser
Scabelle
France, 15th century

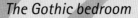

The Gothic bedroom

In the 14th century, bedroom furniture usually consisted of a bed, a chest, a bench, one or two trestle tables for meals, stools and a dresser. The chair, reserved for the lord and his wife, was a 15th-century addition.

As many as eight people could sleep together, on a straw mattress often covered with a feather duvet. They slept in a semi-reclined position as sleeping lying down was associated with death. Beds were therefore quite short. But their often considerable width obliged one to use a pole to put on the sheets. Four-poster beds appeared in royal or princely residences in the 15th century. They were usually placed on a platform and near the fireplace. But the measure of a bedroom's luxury was its textile decoration: silk hangings, often woven with gold and silver thread, and tapestries and blankets lined with marten and sable.

'Annunciation' (detail)
Oil on oak
Flanders, early 16th century

Dresser
Sculpted oak
France, late 15th century
Lower part modern

Scabelle
Oak
France, c.1480

Wool, silk and gold

A selection of wool and silk tapestries, some heightened with gold thread, recalls the essential role of textiles at a time when rooms rarely had fixed decoration. Like the gold grounds of paintings, flowered or millefleur ◉ backgrounds created the illusion of depth until, in the next century, knowledge of perspective spread from Italy. In the early 14th century, Paris and Arras vied for supremacy in tapestry production. The ravages of the Hundred Years War and the invasion of Paris advantaged Arras.

The workshops in Tournai, another important artistic centre, attained the peak of their prosperity in the second half of the 15th century.

The so-called *Scenes from a Novel* tapestry ◉, woven in Paris around 1420, depicts episodes from *The Romance of the Rose*. Its elegant forms and dreamlike compositions are comparable to the International Gothic style then so popular at the great courts of Europe. The museum's tapestry collection, comprising some 200 works from all periods, is one of the five largest in France.

Under Italy's spell

The next room ❹ highlights one of the most fertile periods in art history, but whose dry description as 'transitional', does little justice. During the reign of Louis XII (1498–1515), artists and artisans remained faithful to Late Gothic aesthetics but began adopting Italianate elements such as medallions, scallops, foliation* and arabesques*, laying the foundations for France's Renaissance.

The large oak wardrobe ◉ (France,

c.1510–15), with its huge wrought-iron strap hinges, may have been a liturgical piece—it has the same massive architecture as medieval sacristy furniture. This type of decoration reached France from Italy after Charles VIII's and Louis XII's military campaigns. Its sixteen door panels are sculpted with medallion portraits of eight men and eight women in profile, all wearing extravagant hats. Midway between the medieval dresser and the two-piece cupboard or wardrobe in the School of Fontainebleau style, it marks an important transition in French furniture history.

An oak chest from around the same period has similar, even more colourfully rustic medallions on its front. The antique medals which indirectly inspired them had begun to infiltrate the French artistic vocabulary, but artists were still steeped in the late Gothic aesthetics of the cathedrals.

The Scotch pine friezes from the Castle of Vélez Blanco in Andalusia (1505–20) ◉ (p. 28–29), depicting the triumphs of the Caesars, are inspired by pictures by Mantegna. When these powerful reliefs entered the museum in 1905, they were put in storage and forgotten until their rediscovery in 1992. Their subject matter comes straight from the ancient Rome but their robust, vigorous forms are Renaissance in spirit.

'Scenes from a Novel' tapestry
Wool, silk, gold thread
Paris, c.1420

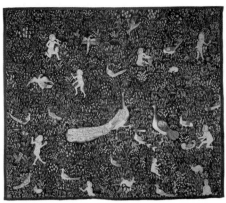

Millefleur tapestry
Wool, silk
South Netherlands, early 16th century

Four-door wardrobe
Sculpted oak with sixteen portrait medallions
France, c.1510–15

p. 28–29
'Triumph of Caesar' (detail)
Scotch pine
Castle of Vélez Blanco
Andalusia, 1505–20

A fantastic bestiary

The display of 13th–16th-century ceramics, enamel and bronze includes secular and liturgical cups, pitchers ◉, goblets and bottles in blown or moulded glass.

The 13th-century Germanic bronze aquamaniles ◉ are a fascinating bestiary of fantastic creatures. Kept in the sacristy, these ewers were used by priests to wash their hands before and after services, and also in the home, until the Renaissance. The word aquamanile is derived from the Latin *aqua* ('water') and *manus* ('hand'). They were heated by the fire and could take the form of an animal, a knight or a half-human half-animal creature and could have several heads.

This fantastic vein and taste for chimerical creatures is characteristic of the medieval imagination. The same bestiary also invaded tapestry, illumination, stained glass and of course architectural sculpture.

One of the finest Limoges champlevé enamel pieces is the gilt copper double-beamed cross ◉ inlaid with coloured glass studs. The emaciated figure of Christ, however, is still Romanesque in style.

Double-beamed cross
Champlevé enamelled and gilt copper,
precious stones, glass studs
Limoges, c.1250

Aquamanile
Chased bronze, handle cast separately
Meuse Valley, 2nd half of the 12th century

Trick jug
Blue-glazed 'Saint-Vérain' stoneware
La Puisaye, c.1430

At the lord's table

The first cookery books, such as Le Viandier, attributed to Taillevent, Charles V's and Charles VI's chef, appeared in the 14th and 15th centuries with the emergence of gastronomy. On feast days, a trestle table with an embroidered linen or damask tablecloth was laid in the great hall of the castle. Guests sat on one side to make serving easier. The host displayed his precious crockery and silverware on a stepped dresser, sometimes protected by a fence. The wine cooler was usually placed on the floor. The food was served in lidded dishes, from which guests served themselves with their fingers or with a knife. The meat was cut up by the squire and served on a dish. People ate off slices of stale bread or platters, and shared drinking cups and goblets.

Dresser
Oak
France, 2nd half of the 15th century

'The Lord's Feast' tapestry
Wool, silk
Brussels, 1510–15

Renaissance

Although marred by the ongoing conflict with Charles V, François I's reign (1515–47) coincided with a period of profound mutation in the arts in France. The wind of change came from Italy, where the radical changes which took place in art and thought in Florence and the great merchant cities in the early 15th century are now collectively known as the Renaissance. In 1532, Rabelais' character Gargantua, writing to his son, said, 'Now is it that the minds of men are qualified with all manner of discipline, and the old sciences revived which for many ages were extinct. Now it is that the learned languages are to their pristine purity restored [...] all the world is full of knowing men, of most learned schoolmasters, and vast libraries.' Facilitated by advances in printing, which reached Paris in 1470, the Renaissance reflected man's immense new appetite for knowledge and steadfast humanism. Writers strove to rival the great Greek and Roman authors, humanists translated the great classical texts, Du Bellay and Ronsard exalted the merits of the French language, and in 1580 Montaigne published his *Essays*.

The traditional architecture of the Loire Valley châteaux was abandoned in new building projects in Île-de-France such as the châteaux de Madrid (destroyed) and Villers-Cotterêts. The medieval Louvre's 'big tower' was demolished in 1528 and the original fortress rebuilt from 1546. Fontainebleau, François I's favourite residence, became a showcase for a new decorative style, pioneered by the two Italian artists who directed work there, Rosso and Primaticcio. With powerful patrons and frequenting humanist circles, great artists acquired the status of creator and eluded the constraints of the guilds.

But there was another, darker side to the new, revitalised culture of the Renaissance. From 1562 to the end of the centuy, the Wars of Religion reaped their toll and tore France apart.

1519
Construction of the Château de Chambord. Death of Leonardo da Vinci.

1529
François I founds the Collège de France.

1539
The Edict of Villers-Cotterêts imposes the use of French in all official and legal documents.

The 'Story of Samuel' window:
'The Capture of the Ark of the Covenant'
(detail, see p. 40)

Renaissance

The phoenix which took flight in Italy in the 15th century and in the rest of Europe several decades later, the Renaissance, was a complete culture inspired by Greek and Roman models which consciously put the medieval era behind it.

Architecture was the first art to adopt the new canons of beauty. And again, its forms—pilasters, columns, entablatures—structured quality furniture. Painters were fond of depicting the new architecture but above all developed an invention which would revolutionise our vision of the world: geometric perspective*.

New perspectives

In this respect, *The Meeting of Jason and Medea* 👁, attributed to the Florentine painter Biagio d'Antonio, is one of the most significant of the many late 15th-century and early 16th-century Italian paintings on display ❺. The centre of the picture is taken up by an elegant hexagonal *tempietto* ('small temple'), whose dome is reminiscent of the Cathedral of Santa Maria dei Fiori in Florence, designed by Brunelleschi. On either side of the legendary couple, the painter has placed two members of the two great Florentine banking families who commissioned the picture. Painted on a poplar wood panel, it was probably originally inset in the panelling at the head of a luxurious bed. Although painters, like sculptors, had at last acquired the status of artist, as opposed to the medieval 'painter of pictures' who, as a craftsman had to obey the regulations of the guilds, they did not consider themselves above undertaking decorative works.

Antiquity reinvented

A very beautiful solid walnut Bolognese *cassone* 👁 dating from the mid-16th century, sculpted with the coat-of-arms of the Malvezzi family, has the then very fashionable form of the antique sarcophagus. The foliation on the central panel, the acanthi on the corners and the lion's paw legs show great familiarity with Roman models.
Vestiges of antique architecture and sculpture, often reused in Christian monuments in Italy, circulated throughout Europe in print form. A fragment of a terracotta bas-relief* 👁, attributed to a follower of Donatello (2nd half of the 15th century), shows how sculpture was gravitating towards more faithful depiction of anatomy. Detaching the profile of the Virgin Mary from the face of the Infant Jesus, the sculptor shows his skill in suggesting perspective. Twenty-four portraits of young people attributed to Bonifacio Bembo, active in Cremona in the second half of the 15th century, were originally set around the spring of a ceiling. They give an idea of the decoration of a *palazzo* in northern Italy around that time.

Venetian supremacy

The glass, ceramics and enamel in the display cases are arranged by material ❻. Venice then dominated European glassmaking. Its influence extended as far as the Netherlands and it is sometimes hard to distinguish glass made in La Serenissima and the finest European

'The Meeting of Jason and Medea'
Attributed to Biagio d'Antonio
Oil on wood
Florence, c.1486

'Virgin and Child'
School of Donatello
Polychromed terracotta
Florence, 2nd half of the 15th century

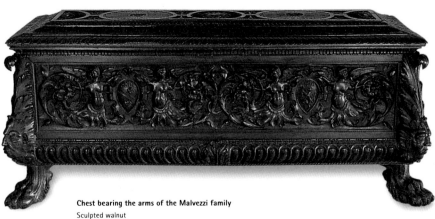

Chest bearing the arms of the Malvezzi family
Sculpted walnut
Bologna, mid-16th century

imitations. The exquisite goblet bearing the arms of the Medicis and belonging to Pope Leon X or Clement VII (1st third of the 16th century), is also enamelled and heightened with gold ☁. The beauty of some pieces, however, is due solely to the virtuosity of the glassblower ☁. Several techniques were often used. The components of the stemmed façon-de-Venise glass (France, late 16th century) were blown, blow-moulded and hot-moulded. Using tongs, the molten glass could be stretched into fanciful forms which were then applied to the stem or chalice.

A curious pitcher, which could be mistaken for an Art Nouveau creation, imitates the richly coloured veins of chalcedony. The pieces in filigree* are even more virtuoso. Glass, because it was costly and fragile, was frequently depicted in the 17th-century still-life genre known as the *vanitas*, symbolising the vanity of all earthly things. In the middle of all these objects attesting to the pomp of aristocratic and princely tables, the *Pieta* ☁ invites us to meditate. The technique of this glazed clay relief by the Buglioni workshop in Florence is very similar to Andrea Della Robbia, to whom it was formerly attributed.

Goblet bearing the arms of a Medici pope
Blown, enamelled and gilt glass
Venice, 1513–34

Stemmed glass
Blown, blow-moulded and hot-worked glass
Façon de Venise
France, late 16th century

'Pieta with Saint Francis and Saint George'
Attributed to the Buglioni workshop
Glazed terracotta
Florence, c.1520

Salt cellar
Pierre Reymond
Enamel, grisaille decoration, gold
Limoges, c.1550

> ## *Painted enamel*
>
> *After a century of neglect, there was a revival in enamel* production in Limoges in the second half of the 15th century, possibly stimulated by Lombard and Venetian enamelwork. Champlevé* enamel was succeeded by painted enamel, for which the Limoges workshops became famous throughout Europe. This technique consisted in applying a uniform coat of enamel to a copper object which, after an initial firing, was then coated with coloured enamel and fired a second time. Metallic oxide pigments were mixed with a silica base which vitrified during firing. Another technique consisted in drawing dark enamel on the copper or white enamel ground. After the first firing, the colouring and modelling was done with translucent enamel, which allowed the dark lines to show through, and light areas could be heightened with gold or silver.*
>
> *Grisaille, first used around 1530, consisted in applying a first coat of dark enamel on which a white coat was painted after firing. The drawing was then engraved by partially removing the white with a metallic burin or spatula. After a second firing, parts could then be modelled with several coats of enamel to achieve gradated effects.*

'The Month of September, the Grape Harvest'
Plate
Pierre Reymond
Grisaille on a black ground, salmon pink, red and gold
Limoges, 1561

Renaissance

The triumph of Limoges

Limoges enamel triumphed again after an eclipse of almost a hundred years, this time not with champlevé* enamel but with painted enamel on copper, a technique pioneered in the city in the 15th century. There was now no raised line between colours.

The museum has a particularly representative collection of this type of enamel. Some pieces, such as the Triptych of the Nativity by the Master of the Louis XII Triptych, are still Gothic in inspiration. A new era began with the arrival in Limoges of Bishop Jean de Langeac, the king's almoner from 1532 to 1541 and a passionate art lover. Italianate motifs such as cabled columns, scalloped canopies and cherubs began to appear. The great enameller Léonard Limosin (before 1577), head of the Limosin dynasty, helped this industry by establishing the fashion for painted enamel at court.

The grisaille* technique, which had been used in stained glass since the 13th century, appeared in the 1530s. Jean Court, Pierre Courteys, Jean II Pénicaud and Pierre Reymond (1513–80) brilliantly exploited its possibilities.

The *Month of September, the Grape Harvest* plate ◉ (p. 37), dated 1561, belongs to a set depicting the months of the year. It was made by the enameller Pierre Reymond from designs by Etienne Delaune, a prolific draughtsman and engraver. This type of plate was not meant to be eaten off but displayed with ceremonial crockery on the shelves of a dresser during banquets.

Jean II Pénicaud painted his *Virgin and Child* ◉ in monochrome on a starry blue ground (16th century). This plaque is a 'kiss of peace', a liturgical object which the congregation were given to kiss as a token of union and mutual charity.

A fine display of Italian faience* illustrates the superiority of the Italian workshops in the finesse of their paste, brilliant glazes and nervous drawing. The five main production centres were Faenza (Emilia), after which this type of glazed earthenware was named, Urbino (Marche) and Deruta ◉ (Umbria). The latter two specialised in metal lustre heightening of the yellows. The speciality of the Castel Durante manufactory was a particular type of dish, often with a blue ground, painted with a bust of a young woman. The *bella,* as she was called, could be portrayed frontally, in profile, like *Hipolita* ◉, attributed to the workshop of Giovanni Maria Vasaro, or three-quarters. Hipolita's extravagant hairstyle matches her sumptuous foliated brocade tunic.

The curiosity cabinet

During the Renaissance, the golden age of humanism, a taste for study and collecting developed in princely and aristocratic circles. This was also the period of the first curiosity cabinets, which mirrored the world in the diversity of man-made and natural objects they contained—everything from the antique medal to a narwhale's tooth. A room ❼ evokes the careful arrangement of one of these rooms devoted to study and delectation. It is decorated with trompe-l'oeil panels (North Italy, late 15th-early 16th century) depicting prelates, scientific and musical instruments ◉, views of cities, landscapes and biblical scenes using the *intarsia** technique. The walls are hung with royal and princely portraits: *Emperor Maximilian of Austria,* his wife *Mary of*

'Nude Woman Standing'
Ceremonial plate
Lustred faience
Deruta, 1st half of the 16th century

Intarsia panel
North Italy
Late 15th–early 16th century

'The Beautiful Hipolita'
Dish
Lustred faience
Castel Durante, early 16th century

'Virgin and Child'
Kiss of peace
Attributed to Jean II Pénicaud
Lustred faience
Limoges, 16th century
17th-century mount

Burgundy, Maria of Austria, Charles V's sister, queen of Hungary and Bohemia then regent of Netherlands (1531), after a portrait by Titian painted in Augsburg in 1548, and *Mary Tudor*, queen of France and Louis XII's last wife. Hanging alongside this gallery of imperial and royal figures are the incisive and penetrating *Portrait of Jacques de Brouillard* ●, baron of Lizy and Montjay (1551), painted in the workshop of François Clouet, miniaturist and 'ordinary painter to the king', and *Portrait of Ambrosius Benson,* painted in Bruges around 1520.

Sumptuous fragments of Brussels tapestries* woven in wool and silk, a French walnut chest decorated with the Labours of Hercules (1546) and several beautiful sculpted panels complete this evocation of this refined environment.

The influence of Fontainebleau

The works and objects in the next room date from highpoint of the French Renaissance, the Second School of Fontainebleau, dominated by Primaticcio, who directed work at the château from 1540 **8**. The new style which developed there under his influence spread via engravings and pervaded all the arts in France, from painting to precious metalwork.

An exceptional set of eight stained glass* windows ●, originally in the Pax Huic Domui academy of painting and drawing in Leyden, depicts the stories of the prophet Samuel, who succeeded Eli as judge of Israel, and the apostle Saint Paul. These windows are attributed to Dirck Crabeth, an artist known from 1520 to

'Portrait of Jacques de Brouillard'
Workshop of François Clouet
Oil on wood
France, 1551

Stained glass window 'The Story of Samuel:
The Capture of the Ark of the Covenant'
Dirck Crabeth and his workshop
Grisaille and silver stain
Leyden, dated 1543

Grotesque decoration

Around 1480, the first visitors to the grotte or caverns of the Golden House ('Domus Aurea'), built by Nero between AD 64 and 68, coined the term grottesco (grotesques) to describe the painted decoration on their walls and vaults. Artists were fascinated by its fanciful mixtures of real and chimerical figures, animals, garlands, foliation and lambrequins. Numerous albums of engravings ensured the circulation of these models throughout Europe. Grotesque decoration spread like wildfire through every domain of Renaissance art: furniture, tapestry, precious metalwork, glass, ceramics and mural decoration. The School of Fontainebleau invented its own sumptuous variations and this stylistic revolution would mark European decoration for several centuries.

Panel with medallions
Walnut
France, 1st half of the 16th century

Grotesques on a yellow ground
Jean Rost, heddle setter
Wool
Florence, 1546–60

1574. The monumental setting for these scenes is an imposing palace loggia with columns, pilasters, niches and arcades.

At the height of the Renaissance, tapestry underwent unparalleled development. The woven border appeared. A tapestry woven in the second half of the 16th century ☻ illustrates the ornamental excesses for which these textile frames became a pretext: garlands of plump fruits and vegetables, ribbons and leatherwork cartouches, etc. Its main subject, *Job Tormented by the Devil*, is restricted to only a small area in the middle by the proliferation of grotesques and medallions on a yellow ground. A tapestry by Jean Rost ☻ (p. 41), woven in Florence in 1546–60, also with a yellow ground, illustrates the triumph of decoration over subject matter. The central allegory, sheltered beneath a whimsical, arbour-like edifice, is merely another motif among the birds in cages, hares, nymphs with breasts like ripe fruit, winged cupids springing out of foliation, lambrequins and leatherwork motifs.

This type of decoration, more airy and less fleshy than at Fontainebleau, is similar to the style of Frans Floris, a Flemish artist who worked in Rome and whose designs circulated via engravings.

The in-the-round and high-relief sculptural decoration on the dresser made in Lyon in the late 16th century ☻ after Hugues Sambin, shows the same hearty appetite for decoration. The vitality of the figures echoes the sonnets of a famous Lyon-born contemporary, Louise Labé, or the voluptuousness of the *Shields* vaunting the beauty of the female body written by Maurice Scève and other writers. The painted and gilded Italian *scabelli* (stools with a back), with their joyous profusion of fruit, foliage and jovial masks, although more crudely sculpted, are just as delightful. In contrast to this decorative euphoria, the wardrobes and two-piece cabinets from Île-de-France ☻, despite their luxurious decoration, reaffirm the primacy of architecture.

One fine example of this typically Second French Renaissance furniture is decorated with gilded figures and inlaid with marble rectangles and medallions contrasting beautifully with the walnut.

There were already similar marble inlays on the facade Pierre Lescot built for François I in the Cour Carrée of Louvre. They are still there today.

The exceptionally sober dresser made in Île-de-France ☻ (p. 45), no doubt in accordance with the wishes of the client, is in the style of Jacques I Androuet Du Cerceau, an architect and engraver in the second half of the 16th century.

Sgabello
Sculpted, painted and gilded walnut
Venice, 16th century

'Job' tapestry
Wool and silk
Netherlands, 2nd half of the 16th century

Two-piece wardrobe
Walnut, gilding, marble inlay
Île-de-France, late 16th century

Dresser
Sculpted walnut
Lyon School, late 16th century

Renaissance

The elegant facade is structured merely by the long fluted columns, panels with simple mouldings and equally simple cornices. By propagating Italian antiquities via his engravings, and also in his famous book, *The Most Excellent Buildings of France* (1576–79), Du Cerceau exercised considerable influence on the art of his time.

The diversification of the form of French chairs began in the 16th century and culminated brilliantly under Louis XV. The *caquetoire* 👁, which, as its French name indicates, was intended to facilitate conversation, widened towards the front to make room for the voluminous *vertugadins* (skirts reinforced with iron hoops, whose maximum circumference was fixed by an edict in 1563) women then wore. The armrests were sometimes set back to create even more space.

Venus

Portrait of Lady in her Bath 👁, attributed to the workshop of François Clouet, gives an idea of a wealthy French interior in the late 16th century.

The robust beauty is portrayed seated in a bathtub draped with white linen. The scene was of course only a pretext to exhibit this beautiful lady's bodily charms. In the Château de Fontainebleau, François had a marble bathroom built and decorated by Primaticcio for his mistress, the Duchess of Etampes.

The famous picture by Lucas Cranach the Elder (1472–1553), *Venus with Cupid Stealing Honey* 👁, introduces us to the atmosphere of refined eroticism at court during this period of rediscovery of the beauty of the human body.

Caquetoire
Oak
France, late 16th century

'Venus with Cupid Stealing Honey'
Lucas Cranach the Elder
Oil on wood
Germany, c.1535

'Portrait of a Lady in her Bath'
Attributed to the workshop of François Clouet
Oil on canvas
France, late 16th century

Dresser
In the style of Jacques I
Androuet Du Cerceau
Walnut, tongue and grooved,
dowelled mortise and tennon joints
Île-de-France,
2nd half of the 16th century

17th century

Henry IV, who came to the throne in 1594, re-established religious peace and endeavoured to make his kingdom prosperous again. The ban on the export of raw materials and the import of luxury products such as silk and tapestries favoured the textile, glass, leather and arms industries.

In 1598, the Edict of Nantes appeased religious tensions but did not diminish the weight of religion in 17th-century society. Artistic developments reflected the revival of the Catholic Church. Columns, angels, pools of light and fingers pointing to the heavens were the grammar of the new Baroque language, which also expressed itself in the construction of triumphal arches for royalty and the engravings of Jacques Callot. Under Louis XIII, France's participation in the Thirty Years War exacerbated its economic problems. Discontent and hostility to royal power mounted in the cities and provinces, leading to numerous jacqueries and culminating with the Fronde from 1648 to 1652.

Artistically, the century was essentially a period of return to order. After the upheavals of the Fronde, Louis XIV built his absolutism on the foundations of the new-found civil peace. Order, good measure and respect for rules manifested themselves not only in politics. From the mid-1630s, the success of Corneille's first tragedies foreshadowed the triumph of the classical ideal. Molière, influenced at the outset by Italian theatre, painted an ironic picture of the morals of his time. In 1664, he performed Tartuffe once, for the king, before it was banned. From the 1660s, Lully dominated the French music scene, establishing the rules for operatic tragedy for a century.

1635
Founding of the Académie Française.

1661
Construction of the
Château de Versailles begins.
It took 50 years and over
30,000 men to build.

1682
The seat of government is
transferred to Versailles.

1692
The Saint-Gobain Company
is founded at Colbert's instigation.
It has the monopoly
on the production of 'façon-de-
Venise' mirrors.

⑨
⑧
⑦
⑥
⑤
④
③
②
①

Wardrobe
(detail, see p. 57)

17th century

The century from Henry IV's assassination in 1610 to the death of Louis XIV in 1715 was rich in stylistic upheavals. It began with the swansong of Mannerism, saw the development of French Classicism and ended at the dawn of Rococo. All roads led to Rome. Artists travelled more widely. Musicians, painters, sculptors and engravers all made the pilgrimage to the Eternal City.

French Prix de Rome laureates stayed at the Mancini Palace, home of the Académie Française in Rome, founded by Colbert in 1666 to cultivate 'the good taste and manner of the Ancients'. Paris also attracted foreign artists, however. In 1621, Queen Marie Médicis commissioned Rubens to decorate a gallery in the Palais du Luxembourg. Later, Bernini himself made a famous trip to Paris, and a host of mainly German and Flemish artists came to work in the Louvre at Henri IV's invitation.

Palatial facades

The first room ❾ evokes the close ties between architectural forms and interior decoration. A new concern for unity emerged out of the will to harmonise furniture's increasingly architectural structure and interior decoration. A new piece of furniture appeared, the cabinet*, a kind of chest with doors and numerous drawers. It had handles and was placed on a table. In the late 16th century, the drawer had already begun replacing the medieval *layette*.

The front of the cabinet made in Augsburg around 1620-30 ◉ (p. 50–51) is like a miniature palace facade, whose majestic forms are decorated with mouldings and motifs sculpted in low relief on the doors. Its sumptuous forms are enhanced by the hardness and blackness of the ebony. Known since the Middle Ages, when it was used for caskets and small objects,

this precious wood began being used for large pieces of furniture in the 17th century.

During the reign of Louis XIII, French joiners working in ebony created a new piece of furniture, adding a base to the cabinet and decorating it with richly sculpted and veneered ebony. In the same room, in the central display case, there are small French and Italian portable cabinets in damascened* iron covered with leather.

An early 17th-century casket ◉ entirely veneered with different-coloured amber*, has bas-reliefs in translucent white amber protected by translucent amber. The working of this fossilised resin attained its highest perfection in the towns on the south coast of the Baltic, where it is found, in Königsberg in East Prussia (now Kaliningrad) and the Pomeranian port of Danzig (Gdansk in modern-day Poland).

The monumental wardrobe with seven columns ◉ (Strasbourg, 1715–20) takes this architectural mimesis to its paroxysm. Its half-columns with Corinthian capitals and cornice with projections could have been taken from the facade of some palace or church. Although the broken arch pediments belong to the Baroque vocabulary, the motifs on the doors come from military architecture.

This wardrobe can be regarded as the swansong of Germanic cabinetmaking in Alsace, which was annexed by France in 1678 and soon became influenced by French styles and techniques. It is also a wonderful testament to the technical mastery of the Strasbourg guilds. It was

Casket
Attributed to the workshop of Georg Schreiber
Limewood, amber veneer, ebony, mica
Königsberg, c.1610–20

Wardrobe with seven columns
Sculpture attributed to Guillaume Le Sage
Oak, pine, sculpted walnut and walnut veneer,
copper, bronze, iron
Strasbourg, 1715–20

made from a design by Johann Loger, altered a year later by his successor Johann Stratz. Breaking with the traditional form of the Renaissance two-piece wardrobe, it is in fact a half-wardrobe corresponding to what we today simply call a wardrobe.

Flemish opulence

Interior of a Palace with Figures ☀, painted by Paul Vredeman De Vries, dated 1616, shows us an opulent, comfortable Dutch interior with panelled walls hung with tapestries, a polychrome marble floor and massive, elegant furniture inspired by Mannerist architecture. The Chinese blue-and-white porcelain attests to the trade with Asia since the founding of the Dutch East India Company in 1603.

Two biblical scenes, *Solomon and the Queen of Sheba* and *The Jugement of Solomon,* also by De Vries, aided by Adriaen Van Nieulandt for the figures, illustrate a genre of urban landscape which first appeared at the court of Emperor Rudolph II in Prague, where De Vries worked with his father Hans.

These episodes illustrating King Solomon's wisdom are merely a pretext for their extraordinary architectural setting of campaniles, loggias and porticos depicted in dramatic perspective. Imaginary architecture becomes almost fantastic in the three pictures by François de Nomé ☀ (1593–after 1630). Painting on an almost black ground, the technique for which he became famous, he depicted a host of edifices and monuments inspired by Antiquity but also Gothic architecture, of which there were magnificent examples at Metz, where he was born, and also in Naples, where he settled around 1613.

These strange moonlit landscapes bathed in a harsh, silvery light evoke Baroque theatre and ephemeral decorations for festivities.

A pair of mid-century giltwood* *bras de lumière* ☀, like the arms of a servant magically emerging from the wall, could almost come from de Nomé's fantastic universe. They also foreshadow the 20th-century universe of the Surrealists: in a legendary scene in Jean Cocteau's *Beauty and the Beast,* based on the fairytale by Charles Perrault, real human arms come out of the wall to light the way for Beauty.

Cartilages and molluscs

A gilt frame sculpted in Utrecht around 1650 heralded an entirely different genre of fantasy. Its humps and uncertain meanders, evoking the flesh of some mollusc, or a monstrous mouth or disturbing eye, are typical of the auricular style. One of the most disconcerting manifestations of late Mannerism, it emerged around 1600 out of the close contacts between Haarlem, an important artistic centre in the North Netherlands, and the Prague of Emperor Rudolph II. It became widespread in northern Europe due to the circulation of albums of prints, but only attained this perfection in the Netherlands.

A few robust chairs and tables are decorated with the cable motif. Woodturning reached the height of its glory in the first half of the 17th century. The motifs were varied: beading, spiral, column, baluster, etc. A mid-century sick chair with turned, Tuscan column legs, illustrates the new concern for comfort. It has padded wings and a reclining back with a wrought-iron mechanism.

Pair of 'bras de lumière'
Sculpted and gilded walnut
France, c.1650–60

'Saint Peter and Saint Paul on the Forum'
François de Nomé
Oil on canvas
Naples, c.1620–30

'Interior of a Palace with Figures'
Paul Vredeman De Vries
Oil on oak
Amsterdam, dated 1616

One of the most striking silver and ceramic pieces on display is a vase from Nevers . Its calabash-shaped form, inspired by Chinese porcelain, is crawling with mythological creatures and the neck is decorated with landscapes. Made in the 1650s, it attests to the quality attained by one of the first French faience workshops.

In the late 16th century, Italian faience makers brought their knowledge to Lyon, Nîmes and Nevers. Although the style of the first Nevers pieces is reminiscent of Urbino majolica, it differs in its use of a 'watered blue' ground and a new colour, manganese violet.

Ivory and tortoiseshell

In the 17th century, with its infatuation with bright, even clashing colours and sumptuous surface effects, there developed a technique derived from the Italian Renaissance intarsia* called marquetry*. Two personalities left an indelible mark on this new technique, which imposed itself in Paris in the mid-century ❿. The first, Pierre Gole (c.1620–84), of Dutch origin, worked for Mazarin and Louis XIV, becoming his cabinetmaker in 1651. His name is associated with a type of very dense floral decoration using violently contrasting colours, tortoiseshell, ivory* and exotic woods such as amaranth*. A casket and stand attributed to his workshop  is an example of the extremely stylistically affected furniture in vogue in the mid-17th century.

The second, André-Charles Boulle (1642–1732), was also born into a family from the Netherlands. Johann Bolt, his father, was born in the duchy of Gelder in the lower Rhine Valley. In 1672, Boulle became

Calabash vase
Faience, high-fired, polychrome decoration
Nevers, c.1650

Casket and stand
Attributed to Pierre Gole
Pine, tortoiseshell, ivory, tinted ivory,
tinted bone, ebony and hardwood veneer
Paris, c.1655–65

Casket and stand
(detail, see p. 54)

Painting in wood

The Art of marquetry* developed in Italy in the 14th century. It consists in applying elements cut out of thin sheets of wood to a surface to create ornamental or figurative compositions. In the 17th century, this technique evolved considerably with the use of the saw, more precise than the chisel, for cutting. Known as 'painting in wood', it was ideal for floral compositions, animals, figures and decorative motifs. In the late 17th century, 'bois des îles' (island wood) became popular: amaranth* from Guyana, snakewood from the West Indies, amboina from the Moluccas, rosewood* from Brazil, and sandalwood and rosewood from India. These woods were sometimes inlaid with bone, ivory* and metal.

Boulle marquetry, named after André-Charles Boulle, who was appointed 'ordinary cabinetmaker to the king' in 1672, was in fact a technique invented in Germany. It consists in simultaneously cutting out superimposed sheets of tortoiseshell and metal (tin, copper, brass) to obtain the same motif twice: the first, positive or 'in part', in metal on a tortoiseshell ground; the second, negative or 'in counterpart', in tortoiseshell on a metal ground.

Cabinet
Pine, walnut, limewood, amaranth, box, yew,
pear, sycamore, ebony and bone marquetry
Paris, c.1670

Design for an eight-legged desk
Attributed to André-Charles Boulle
Red chalk
Paris, c.1700–1710

'ordinary cabinetmaker to the king'. Although he did not invent it, he perfected a type of extremely ornate marquetry in which copper and tin arabesques stand out on a wood or tortoiseshell ground within a shiny black ebony frame. His pieces are always decorated with gilt* bronze. This use of superimposition was widely copied by his contemporaries. A very beautiful two-piece cabinet or *cabinet en armoire* ◉ (Paris, c.1670–80) plays on the contrast between the silvery reflections of the tin and the dark, warm veins of the rosewood*.

A large cabinet ◉ (p. 55), whose six legs have diagonal cross-struts (Paris, c.1670), has large floral pictures in different-coloured marquetry on its two doors. No metal was used here, or even ivory (replaced by bone) and giltwood replaced bronze. The decorative effect of this 'element by element' marquetry is created by using different species of exotic and indigenous woods: box, yew, pear, amaranth, ebony, sycamore* and walnut, and burnt wood for the ground. This type of piece was extremely popular in France, England and Holland. Despite successive wars, the stylistic cohesion between these three countries remained strong.

The reign of Flora

The craze for floral decoration eclipsed all references to Antiquity except for the stylised acanthus* leaves mingling with the flowers around the borders. The same was true in painting, with the 'blooming' of the floral still life. From the 16th century the great collectors brought plants imported from the East, including the tulip, for fantastic sums. A pair of Delft faience pyramid vases ◉ (c.1700–25) evokes the 'tulipmania' that swept the Netherlands.

Flowers invaded all refined everyday objects. The enamelled copper goblet and saucer ◉ attributed to Noël II Laudin (Limoges, c.1700) are decorated remarkably economically with a few flowers tied with a ribbon. Their refined simplicity contrasts with the affectation of the antique heroines they surround, then known as 'stout women': Semiramis, Pauline and Artemis, copied from engravings by Claude Vignon.

Artful calligraphy

The arabesques* which pervaded the decorative arts in the 17th century and early 18th century were dubbed the 'new grotesques' ⑪. Although drawing heavily on the fantastic repertoire of the Roman grotesques reinvented by the Renaissance artists, they have a character all their own. Dissociated from their classical forebears, they acquired a new graphic unity.

Although one still encounters all kinds of figures, men, children and animals, they tend more towards a kind of abstract calligraphy. Due to their small scale, these arabesques had to be highly stylised, with a few birds or a fantastic animal here and there, and often, as in Berain's work, a human figure, depicted full length and no longer merely from the waist up.

An extraordinary double harpsichord lid ◉ (p. 58), painted on a gold ground, shows the vitality of these arabesques with figures. The Triumph of Music in the middle appears to be taking place on a tray covered with a cloth with lambrequins.

Goblet and saucer
Attributed to Noël II Laudin
Painted enamel on copper
Limoges, c.1700

Pyramid vase
Attributed to the De Roos manufactory
Faience, high-fired polychrome decoration
Delft, c.1700–25

Two-piece cabinet
Oak and pine, tin marquetry on an
amaranth ground, chased and gilt bronze
Paris, c.1670–80

'A la Berain'

Jean Berain (1637–1711) was the chief instigator of the blooming of arabesque decoration in the second half of the century. As ornamentalist and draughtsman to the king's Cabinet, he produced designs to be executed by others. His realm of influence was immense, from the opera to state funerals to clothes and precious metalwork. His designs circulated via engravings, and were to be seen everywhere from the lid of a box to an ornamental flower bed.

Gilded* mirrors, *torchères,* chandeliers and even the bases of console tables and massive armchairs in sculpted and gilt wood during the second half of Louis XIV's reign followed the caprices of the new forms in vogue ⓬. The back-painted glass frame of a monumental mirror with a scrolled pediment ◉ (early 18th century) is entirely covered with 'à la Berain' arabesques in gold on a red lacquer ground, creating the impression of Boulle marquetry.

A ceiling ◉ painted a few years later for the Hôtel de Verrüe, attributed to Claude III Audran, Watteau's master, deploys above us a network of fanciful, airily graceful motifs, a veritable ornamental potpourri peopled with birds and monkeys. And no animal could be more suited to this fanciful decoration than that comical tightrope walker, the ape—so ideally suited that it gave rise to a genre. 'Singerie' portrayed monkeys in human costume, 'aping' the occupations of elegant life. Ceramic* decoration, usually in blue on a white

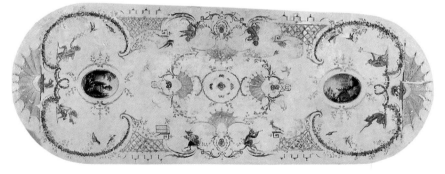

Painted ceiling with singerie decoration
Attributed to Claude III Audran
Oil on plaster mounted on canvas
Paris, c.1720

Double harpsichord lid
Paint and oil-based gilding on oak
Paris?, c.1690–1700

Jean Berain

Mirror (detail)
Saint-Gobain royal manufactory
Silvered glass mirror, pine back, sculpted and gilt
limewood?, eglomise glass
Glass decoration and assembly, Paris, c.1700–10

Jean Berain (1638–1711) was born into a family of arquebusiers in Lorraine, and at nineteen published his album Divers Pieces Useful for Arquebusiers. *He rapidly established himself as one of the most prolific ornamentalists of the 17th century. Appointed designer to Louis XIV in 1674, he organised fêtes and entertainments, designed their decorations and costumes and even the feasts served at them.*

His main claim to fame, however, is a Renaissance motif, the grotesque*. Rebaptised arabesque*, this new ornamental style pervaded all domains of interior decoration. His compositions are peopled with comical little characters or allegorical figures portrayed beneath fanciful porticos and surrounded by a dense network of arabesques, ribbons and interlacing bands creating a highly musical harmony. Berain published numerous engravings, via which his style circulated, and shortly after his death an album of his entire œuvre was published.

Large dish
Clérissy workshop
Faience, high-fired decoration
Moustiers-Sainte-Marie, c.1730

Horseman in caroussel costume
Jean Berain
Pen and ink, bistre wash, sepia highlights
Paris, c.1685

ground, became a favourite medium for this highly graphic decorative genre. Rouen and Nevers but above all Moustiers-Sainte-Marie ● developed this style in the first third of the 18th century. In the 1670s, the Clérissy factory attained great refinement in its creamy paste and dazzling white enamel, and a then unrivalled perfection in its drawing.

'A la Berain' decoration spread with the movements of artists, to Germany, Italy and especially Spain, at the Alcora manufactory ●.

The Saint-Cloud manufactory, founded in 1666, produced innumerable variations ●. In the last decade of the century, under the entrepreneurial directorship of Pierre Chicaneau, it became the crucible of the porcelain* industry in France along with the Poterat manufactory in Rouen. They still produced only soft-paste porcelain as the kaolin used by the Chinese was still unknown in Europe. This privately-owned manufactory benefited from the unofficial protection of the Duke of Orléans, Louis XIV's brother, who lived in the neighbouring château.

Vase
Soft-paste porcelain, underglaze blue decoration
Saint-Cloud manufactory, c. 1695–1700

Dish
Francisco O. Grangel, painter
Faience, high-fired polychrome decoration
Alcora manufactory
Spain, c.1730

Fireplace
Attributed to the Clérissy workshop
Faience, high-fired decoration
Moustiers-Sainte-Marie, c.1720–30

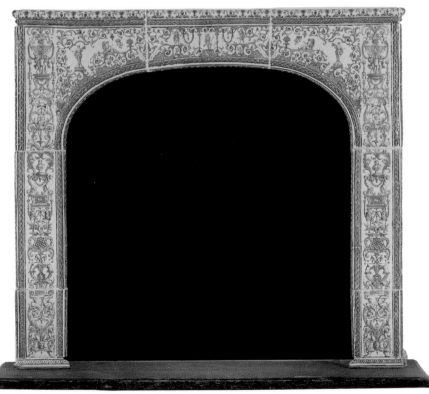

18th century

Was the philosophy of the Enlightenment born in Newton's England, Leibniz's Germany or Huygen's Holland? One thing is certain, its faith in progress through science and its ideals of equality and liberty seduced the whole of 18th-century Europe. In Voltaire's France its influence was exceptional. Philosophers sought to replace the darkness of fanaticism with the light of reason. Royal absolutism began to be criticised. In 1734, Voltaire sung the praises of the English institutions. In 1748, Montesquieu published *The Spirit of Laws,* in which he advocated a monarchy founded on the separation of executive, legislative and judiciary powers. Jean-Jacques Rousseau saw the return to the simplicity of nature as an antidote to the corruption of society. In *The Social Contract,* he imagined an ideal, just and legitimate society. The literary Salons propagated these new ideas.

Reflecting man's new relationship with nature, the landscaped garden appeared in Britain at the beginning of the century. It was transformed when it reached France, Italy, Germany and Russia after 1760. Inspired by the pictures of Claude Lorraine, it was a reaction to the formal design of the French-style garden.

Gluck's opera *Alceste,* premièred in Vienna in 1767, heralded the advent of a new, tragic and grandiose style of music. In Paris, where Rameau's brilliant, refined scores were still considered the paragon of excellence, this revolution prompted a legendary quarrel.

In the theatre, the grace and spirit of the century were epitomised by Marivaux's intrigues. The games of hide-and-seek of his characters, their giddy amorous delights and inconstancy echoed the caprice of rococo.

Panel of the Lacquer Study in the Hôtel Du Châtelet
(detail, see p. 79)

1751
Beginning of the publication
of Diderot and d'Alembert's
Encyclopaedia, compiled in the spirit
of the Enlightenment.

1762
Louis XV builds
the Petit Trianon in the
new Neoclassical style.

1783
Pilâtre de Rozier makes the first
voyage in a hot-air balloon; the first
trial of a steamboat by Jouffroy
d'Abbans in Lyon.

18th century

The century of the Enlightenment was also the century of conversation and pleasure, and, as Talleyrand famously wrote, the century of 'sweetness of living'—at least for the elite. Europe spoke French and looked to Paris for new fashions and styles. Mirabelles, Sans-Soucis, Hermitages, Montplaisirs and Solitudes sprang up from Stockholm to Saint Petersburg to Palermo. Never would Paris be so revered, imitated and envied.

The pomp of the Régence

By the beginning of the 18th century, the sumptuous, pompous style of the reign of Louis XIV had begun to soften. During the Régence (1715–23), the court left Versailles for Paris. The great lords, financiers and nouveau riche built themselves vast, comfortable, luxuriously furnished mansions, and Watteau set his fêtes galantes in the golden shade of imaginary parks.

The vogue for the arabesque endured, losing nothing of its vigour. A large gilt oak console table ☻ (c.1710–20) with a heavy Rance marble top illustrates the triumph of decoration over structure ⓭.

The table's lines dissolve in the interplay of curves, crosiers, flowers, fantastic animals, chimeras and dragons. But this artful disorder does not compromise its solidity. The four legs are held together by robust cross-struts, whose intersection serves as a base for a vase. Bronze, less limited by structural constraints, can be shaped into the most daring forms. The tortoiseshell and copper marquetried structure of the wall clock ☻ (p. 71) made by Charles Cressent around 1733 is concealed behind a gilt bronze facade with powerful dragons.

This creature is also to be seen on the monumental two-piece dresser decorated with the monogram of its owner surrounded by hunting scenes. One can easily compare such decorative extravagances with contemporary costume. In *Portrait of Octave-Alexandre de Nédonchel as a Hunter* ☻ painted by Jean-Baptiste Oudry in 1713, the pyramidal wig, tunic with flared sleeves, wide turned-cuffs and waistcoat negligently open to show off a baggy shirt are just as overelaborate. Montesquieu denounced the height of wigs during the Régence in his *Persian Letters,* published in 1721: 'Sometimes wigs get unnoticeably higher, then a revolution brings them down all at once.'

Faience* production developed in the major towns due to the sumptuary laws, but in the first third of the century Rouen was incontestably the most active and innovative centre. The colour harmonies obtained by high-firing became subtler due to the mastery of red (the famous Armenian bole), and new ornamental compositions free of all foreign influence appeared, such as the radiating motif and niello decoration. Genuine faience sculptures like the classically-inspired busts of Cleopatra and Mark Anthony were produced in Marseille, Rouen ☻ and Nevers.

In contrast, it is a baroque wind that swirls the drapery in *The Four Seasons* ☻, attributed to the workshop of the Genovese sculptors Filippo and Domenico Parodi (c.1700–20). Spectacular in their radical contrast between gold and black, they stand on rocky mounds which have all the power of Bernini.

In the Prints and Drawings Room ⓮, drawings or ornaments and designs for furniture and objets d'art are shown on a rotary basis.

Baluster vase
Attributed to the Guillebaud workshop
Faience, high-fired polychrome decoration
Rouen, c.1720–30

'Winter'
Workshop of Filippo and Domenico Parodi
Wood painted black and gilded, wood base
imitating marble and porphyry
Genoa, c.1700–20

**'Portrait of Octave-Alexandre de Nédonchel
as a Hunter'**
Jean-Baptiste Oudry
Oil on canvas
Paris, dated 1713

Console table
Sculpted and gilt oak, red Rance marble
Paris, c.1710–20

The museum's comprehensive collection includes works by many of greatest French and European artists and ornamentalists.

The glassware display includes several pieces attributed to Bernard Perrot , the great glassmaker during the reign of Louis XIV and inventor of the process for making mirror glass which enabled the founding of the Saint-Gobain royal manufactory.

Around a polychrome dolphin table decoration ●, are forms and types of decoration characteristic of French glass production in the late 17th and early 18th century.

Stemmed glass
Blown and hot-formed glass
France, façon de Venise, 17th century

Golds and mirrors

The Gilt Study in the Hôtel de Rochegude ● (p. 68–69) is a provincial, Provençal echo of the great decorations in the royal residences in Paris ⑯. In 1730, Laurent-Joseph de Rochegude bought the mansion in Avignon now named after him, but this study was commissioned by its previous owner, André de Paÿs des Hoirs, around 1720. Unusually, its decoration was not entrusted to a local artisan but to a sculptor of the King's Buildings, Thomas Lainé. After working at Versailles he moved to Avignon in 1714, bringing with him the innovative style of the great royal projects.

The distinctive features of this study are its mixture of painted and sculpted decoration, the variety of ornamental motifs, and the richness and abundance of the gilding. The techniques and materials used are local ones: walnut instead of oak and gilding applied using oil not water. The large mirrors reflect the brilliant gilding. Until the 1660s, mirrors were never large and imported from Venice, but from

Dolphin
Table decoration
Bernard Perrot
Glass, blown, hot-moulded and hot-formed
Orléans, late 17th century

Jug
Antoine Bailly, silversmith
Silver, amaranth wood
1753–54

Tea, coffee or chocolate?

Chocolate was the first exotic beverage to reach Europe. It came from America, first to Spain, in the mid-16th century. Queen Marie-Thérèse, Louis XIV's wife, contributed to its success in France. Tea and coffee became popular first in Netherlands. As these drinks were initially considered medicinal, they were sold only by apothecaries. The publication of Pierre Masson's The Perfect Café Owner, or the Art of Preparing Tea, Coffee and Chocolate [...], consecrated their status as gourmet delicacies. Recipients were designed for them, with specific spouts and handles for each drink, and the lid of the chocolate pot had a hole in it for the wooden whisk.

The first coffee houses opened in England, then in Paris in the late 17th century. On the eve of the Revolution there were already 900 in Paris.

**Coffeepot from an album
of silverware designs**
c.1690–1700

p. 68-69
**Panelling of the Gilt Study
in the Hôtel de Rochegude**
Thomas Lainé, architect
Limewood, pine, mirror glass
Avignon, c.1720

1692, the Saint-Gobain royal manufactory began producing large mirrors. They were extremely costly and it is the size of this study's mirrors rather than its gilding which gives a measure of the wealth of its owner.

Leather, velvet and tapestry

The few chairs which still have their original covering are priceless testaments to the skill and effects sought by the upholsterers of the period ⑰. In the 17th and 18th centuries, the upholsterer's role in a chair's final appearance was often more important than the joiner's, yet only the latter can be identified today by his stamp. Different materials were used. Leather, used widely in the 17th century, was employed in the next century solely for chairs with specific uses such as desk chairs, sick chairs ◉ and dining-room chairs, whose solidity was more important than their luxurious finish. The fabrics used were velvets, often embossed, needlepoint tapestry, Gobelins or more frequently Aubusson tapestry, and occasionally Savonnerie tapestry. Chairs could also be caned or 'darkened with cane', using a technique developed in the Netherlands and already widespread in England under Charles II. They often had a morocco leather or tapestry cushion.

Lady at her Dressing Table ◉ by Guillaume Voiriot gives an idea of the most delicate textile decoration of the period: the gathered lace is draped over the dressing table or *toilette*—the French word for a table with a mirror on which one put makeup, powder and brushes. It was always luxuriously covered, as both women and men of quality often received lovers, friends and relations while they were putting on their

Sick chair
Beech, box, iron, bronze, leather
Paris?, c.1710

'Lady at her Dressing Table'
Guillaume Voiriot
Oil on canvas
Paris, c.1760

Wall clock
Charles Cressent
Blackened oak, brown tortoiseshell and brass
marquetry, copper, chased and gilt bronze
Paris, c.1733–35

Charles Cressent

Charles Cressent (1685–1768), cabinetmaker to the Regent, was one of the most brilliant artists of the first half of the 18th century. In 1719, he took over the workshop of Joseph Poitou, where he had served his apprenticeship. Like Boulle he decorated his furniture with highly ornate gilt bronzes: trophies, grotesque figures, groups of children, etc. These stood out against geometric amaranth* and satine* wood veneer. The grandson of a cabinetmaker in Amiens and son of François Cressent, sculptor to the king, he was himself also a sculptor, chaser and founder. The smiling female busts embellishing the corners of his flat desks and chests of drawers are some of the finest creations of the period.

He created numerous models for clocks and firedogs, whose tempered fancifulness accompanied the emergence of Rococo.

His most prestigious clients included Louis XV, the king of Portugal, the Elector of Bavaria, and the great financiers.

Wardrobe
(detail, see p. 73)

Window catch
Charles Cressent
Chased and gilt bronze
Paris, 1745–49

makeup, beauty spots, brushing their hair and powdering themselves.

The art of parquetry

Until the mid-18th century, cabinetmakers often decorated furniture using a technique called parquetry ⑮. The decorative effect of this type of veneer is obtained using geometric compositions that vary according to the way their elements, in a variety of precious woods, are cut and their grain. Kingwood*, with its magnificent dark grain and violet red colour, was highly prized. It was used on the large wardrobe ● attributed to Joseph Poitou, the famous cabinetmaker whose workshop Charles Cressent took over in 1719 when he married his widow—a practice then common in joiners' and cabinetmakers' workshops.

This wardrobe illustrates the spectacular effects obtained with artfully composed parquetry. The kingwood is a perfect counterpoint to the gilt* bronzes, probably by Cressent himself, who was a sculptor before he was a cabinetmaker.

The exceptional chest of drawers with corner cupboards ●, nearly three metres long, is veneered with mosaic rosewood parquetry. Despite its huge size, the daring cabinetmaker, who did not stamp this piece (it was not obligatory to stamp one's work until 1743), gave it only four legs – but sturdy ones, with powerful bronze bear's claws.

It has four drawers and cupboards with one door on either side. This chest of drawers is reminiscent of the pieces Antoine-Robert Gaudreaus made for the Royal Furniture Repository.

The chest of drawers was still in its infancy. Probably invented by Boulle, it appeared in the late 17th century, when the popularity of the cabinet was waning. It is in fact a metamorphosis of the eight-legged desk (baptised the 'Mazarin' desk in the 19th century, despite it having appeared after his death), and was originally called the desk-cum-chest of drawers. Its place was in the bedroom or study. In the 18th century, its fragile veneered or marquetried top was replaced with marble—more durable and just as elegant.

Examples of the various effects obtained using parquetry are displayed on shelves: diamond, butterfly wing, mosaic, etc.

In the mid-18th century, parquetry was often used with marquetry, which had come back into fashion. The pair of corner cabinets by Christophe Wolff ● are decorated with light, flowering foliation in cross-grain cut* kingwood on a light satine* wood ground with a contrasted, light and dark grain.

Corner cabinet
Christophe Wolff
Oak, kingwood and satine wood marquetry,
Chased and gilt bronze, Brèche d'Alep marble
Paris, c.1750

Wardrobe
Joseph Poitou, cabinetmaker
Charles Cressent, bronze founder
Oak, kingwood veneer, chased and gilt bronze
Paris, c.1710–20

Chest of drawers with corner cupboards
Oak and pinewood frame, rosewood and watered walnut veneer,
chased and gilt bronze, red Rance marble
Paris, c.1725

18th century

Chicory leaves and bat's wings

In the 1730s, all the ingredients of the joyous stylistic feast called rocaille came together: agrafes, asymmetric seashells, scatterings of flowers, operatic rocks, leaves curling into crosiers, chicory leaves, bat's wings, twined branches and languid palm trees ⑱. Matter, in a state of fusion, seemed to obey the sculptor's fingers: one no longer constructed, one modelled, kneaded.

The great bronze founder Jacques Caffiéri ☜ (1678–1755) transformed his firedogs into gallinaceans with human heads riding headless and tailless ornaments rearing like some strange crustacean, and called them *The Cockerel and the Hen*. In his mythological pictures, François Boucher ☜ sits his buxom divinities on swirling clouds. Everything from the door handle to crockery was subjected to extraordinary metamorphoses. The silversmith Claude Duvivier ☜ turned Juste-Aurèle Meissonnier's feverish forms into silver. Meissonnier, a painter, architect, engraver, sculptor and silversmith, was above all a great creator of forms and largely contributed to the triumph of the rocaille style in Paris in the 1730s. Engravings of his designs circulated widely.

The *Duplessis* sauceboat ☜ (p. 77), made at the Vincennes manufactory in 1756, fringed with gold and agitated by blue waves, is like some fairytale seashell. A small coral branch confirms its marine origin. By that time, Buffon had already published several volumes of his *Natural History,* and Linné, studying the sexuality of flowers, had laid the foundations of his famous classification.

At a time when science was comparing, ordering and labelling the natural world,

decorative art was inventing a parallel one. Never had a style seemed as natural and spontaneous yet distanced itself so much from nature. Jean-Claude Duplessis, the king's bronze founder and precious metalsmith, was appointed artistic director of the Vincennes manufactory and remained in charge after it was moved to Sèvres in 1756. And like his great rival Meissonnier, he was born in Turin.

Workshops like the Pont-aux-Choux ☜ *terres d'Angleterre** manufactory, in Paris' Marais quarter and named after a bridge across the market gardens there, adopted this formal vocabulary more prudently, retaining a certain symmetry. Its generous, simple forms, like a Chardin still life, imitated silverware.

Abroad, rocaille became rococo, abandoning skilfully balanced compositions for strange, colourful, outrageous assemblages. A Venetian chest of drawers ☜, painted with bouquets of flowers and varnished, swells its chest like the frog in the fable. The group of elegant hunters tottering on a white and gold terrace was modelled around 1760 by Franz-Anton Bustelli at the Neudeck manufactory in Bavaria, which moved a few years later to Nymphenburg. Rococo ornament spread to architecture.

Nevers glass figurines ☜ (p. 76) were impervious to all fashions except the perennial vogue for the picturesque. *The Four Seasons* is a particularly remarkable example of these miniature sculptures modelled from sticks of glass using an enameller's lamp.

Pair of firedogs
Jacques Caffiéri
Chased and gilt bronze
Paris, c.1735

'The Forge of Vulcan'
François Boucher
Oil on canvas, sketch in grisaille
Paris, 1756

Terrine
Faience
Pont-aux-Choux manufactory, c.1750

Candelabrum
Juste-Aurèle Meissonnier, designer
Claude Duvivier, silversmith
Cast and chased silver
Paris, 1734–35

Chest of drawers with side doors and writing surface
Pine, sculpted, painted and gilt decoration, marble top
Venice, c.1750–60

A theatrical China

The insatiable appetite for the picturesque inevitably led several painters,
sculptors and ornamentalists to the
beauties of the Middle Kingdom, to its
grimacing magots*, long-moustachioed
and long-sleeved mandarins ☜. But the
China of these chinoiseries ⑲ was to the
real China what Mozart's *The Abduction
from the Seraglio* is to the Sublime Door:
a marvellous comic opera. Chinamen with
parasols climbed to the summits of gilt*
bronze wall clocks (those of François
Autray, for instance, made in Paris around
1740), while others fished, drank tea or
made music, as in Boucher's compositions, which circulated widely as prints
and were often copied.

But for the illusion to be perfect, the
real had to be mixed with the imaginary.
Oriental vases and magots imported from
China and Japan were given sumptuous
gilt bronze mounts, and were soon joined
by imitations produced in the porcelain
manufactories at Saint-Cloud, Mennecy
and Chantilly, and to a lesser extent at
Vincennes ☜ and Sèvres ☜.

European artisans such as Johann Joachim
Kaendler at the Meissen manufactory
appropriated the oriental bestiary of par-
rots, armadillos, elephants and monkeys.
Delft faience, a pioneer in this field, pursued the Chinese vein and was joined in
this by the manufactories at Rouen and
Sinceny.

Lacquer* panels were imported by the
shipload. They were cut up and incorpo-
rated into chests of drawers and writing
desks but also used as complete pieces.
The museum has a unique collection of
red and gold lacquer panels framed with
rosewood from one of the finest Chinese
decors of the time: the Lacquer Study in

'The Four Seasons'
Opaque white glass modelled with an enameller's lamp;
turned and gilt wood base
Probably Nevers, 2nd half of the 18th century

Potpourri with magots with moveable heads
Soft-paste porcelain, stanniferous glaze,
underglaze polychrome decoration
Chantilly manufactory, c.1740

Stemmed glass with Chinese decoration (detail)
Wheel-engraved glass
Bohemia, c.1730

'Duplessis' sauceboat
Jean-Claude Duplessis, designer
Soft-paste porcelain, polychrome decoration
with gold heightening
Vincennes manufactory, 1756

The secret of porcelain

European ceramicists fascinated by the porcelain imported from China tried to discover its secrets from the late 15th century. A century later, 'Medici porcelain' was produced for a short time in Florence. Without kaolin, the white clay used in China from the 12th century, manufactories developed various types of 'soft-paste' porcelain. The difficulty consisted in obtaining translucency after firing. To achieve this, a frit (a vitreous silica-based mixture) was added to the white marl (calcareous clay). The secret lay in the composition of the frit. Experiments were carried out again in the late 17th century, first at the faience manufactory in Rouen then at Saint-Cloud. In the next century, Vincennes elevated the technique to the peak of its perfection from 1740. After it moved to Sèvres in 1756, this manufactory became the largest in Europe.

In 1708, the discovery of kaolin in Saxony heralded the beginnings of hard-paste porcelain* in Europe, for which the Meissen manufactory became famous. In France, the first kaolin deposits were discovered near Limoges in 1765.

Wine glass cooler
Soft-paste porcelain, polychrome decoration
with gold heightening
Vincennes manufactory, c.1749–53

Water pitcher and 'water leaf' bowl
Soft-paste porcelain, polychrome decoration
with gold heightening
Sèvres royal manufactory, 1756–57

the Hôtel Du Châtelet ◉ (p. 79) (now the Labour Ministry), built in rue de Grenelle in Paris in 1770 by Mathurin Cherpitel. This imported decor is furnished with a small chest of drawers, Martin-varnished* with a red ground by Dubois, a drop-front writing desk attributed to Adrien Faizelot Delorme, varnished in blue and the property of Madame de Pompadour at Bellevue, and a Coromandel-lacquered (Chinese-lacquered) chest of drawers by Desmoulin. The forms of the writing desk by Jean-François Leleu (Paris, c.1765), at the frontier of chinoiserie and rocaille, are almost anthropomorphic. The craze for lacquer was such that even the ceramics manufactories at Delft, Rouen ◉ and Sèvres tried to imitate this mysterious technique.

'A la capucine'

After this bevy of colour and exoticism, a dining room with à la capucine (polished) oak panelling is the sober setting for selections of tableware, glass, ceramics and silverware displayed on rotary basis ⓴. The panelling, originally in a Paris mansion built around 1730, is so brilliantly sculpted that one wonders how the term 'à la capucine' (in the Capuchin style) could be an allusion to the strict rules these monks lived by, going barefoot and bareheaded in winter. The supposed 'poverty' of this unpainted wood is merely a mask for the utmost elegance. In the jargon of the time, the word capucin also meant exaggerated devotion...

Just as in the 18th century chairs diversified to adapt to every occupation and time of day, new rooms such as the boudoir, a room adjoining the bedroom, began to appear in private apartments. The panelling painted with La Fontaine's fables ◉, attributed to Christophe Huet ㉒, was originally in the boudoir of Madame Dangé, wife of a farmer general who in 1750 bought the former Hôtel de Villemaré in place Louis-le-Grand (now place Vendôme). When in the mid-19th century the building was allocated to Paris's military administration, the pink and green panelling was covered with gilt mouldings. During its recent restoration it was decided to only partially restore it to its 18th-century state to show the evolution of taste and the building's change in use.

A new classicism

People gradually grew tired of the spiritual contortions of rococo and under Louis XV there was a return to classical roots and more sober forms ㉑. Just as the Louis XV style began during the Régence, Louis XVI aesthetics emerged during the reign of the Bien-Aimé. The rims of chairs ◉ were no longer sculpted but merely moulded. The intersections between the seat and legs were decorated with squares sculpted with quatrefoils*. The curves of table legs were attenuated into long tensile lines. Flowered marquetry in jig-saw cut frames were superseded by more geometric compositions, three-dimensional cubes and taught interlacing. Symmetry came back into favour as would the straight line. These calmed-down forms were decorated with à la grecque (in the Greek style) motifs, although these were in fact derived from Roman decoration: rows of piastres, beads, acanthus leaves*, Greek fret, ovi, garlands of flowers, fluting, candelabras, fasces, profile medals and draped figures.

Terrine in the form of a turkey
P. Mombaers workshop
Faience, high-fired polychrome decoration
Brussels, c.1760

Saucer
Faience, high-fired polychrome decoration
Rouen, c.1725–30

'A la reine' armchair
Jean-Baptiste Gourdin
Beech and walnut, moulded, sculpted and painted
Paris, c.1765–70

Panel from the Lacquer Study in the Hôtel Du Châtelet
Chinese lacquer, red ground, black and gold decoration;
amaranth frame; painting imitating rosewood
Paris, c.1771

**Panelling from the Fables Study
in the Hôtel Dangé (detail)**
Sculpted and painted oak
Paris, 1750–55

It was a second-hand vocabulary, mostly borrowed from the solemn art of the reign of Louis XIV. This classical reaction expressed itself first in a tribute to the art of the French architecture of the Grand Siècle. The pavilions on place Louis XV (place de la Concorde), designed by Jacques-Ange Gabriel and partly inspired by Perrault's colonnade in the Louvre, are a fine example.

He also designed the Ecole Militaire, which Madame de Pompadour wanted to be the greatest monument erected during Louis XV's reign. Its dome is based on that of the Pavillon de l'Horloge in Louis XIV's Louvre. Cabinetmakers now decorated their furniture with bronzes made in the workshops of Boulle and Cressent. Around 1760, Philippe-Claude Montigny placed a figure of Danae, copied from a wall clock by Cressent, in the middle of a soberly classical drop-front writing desk ☜, and decorated the corners with agrafes inspired by Boulle.

Antiquity reinterpreted

There was no concern for archaeological accuracy in the use of Greek-style motifs, not even after the discovery of the ruins of Pompeii and Herculaneum, the ancient city excavated on Charles III's orders from 1738.

In his *Familiar Letters from Italy*, Président de Brosses wrote on 24 November 1739: 'day after day, we discover new things. The most precious is part of an antique fresco painting [...]. You know how what little we have left of antique painting makes us value what we have'. Pompeii was also excavated, first in 1748, then more systematically from 1755. In the 1760s, both sites, near Naples, became obligatory destinations on the 'Grand Tour' which young British aristocrats and the wealthy now made of Europe and particularly Italy. This new appetite for antique sculpture, painting and architecture was wetted by publications by artists, archaeologists and art lovers such as Abbé de Saint-Non, a friend of Fragonard.

The new style pervaded all the arts and influenced every aspect of the interior from wall decoration to silverware. *Pygmalion and Galatea* ☜, sculpted by Etienne-Maurice Falconet and reproduced in biscuit* by the Sèvres manufactory, could be an allegory to this renaissance. It was enthusiastically hailed by Diderot as the manifesto of the new style at the 1763 Salon. Like the sculptor Pygmalion, who fell in love with an ivory statue he carved and persuaded Venus to bring her to life, the art of Antiquity was reborn in contemporary creations thanks to the passion of archaeologists and the cultivated elite.

Greece, on the other hand, still under Turkish domination and seldom visited, was known mainly through James Stuart and Nicholas Revett's monumental and pioneering, *The Antiquities of Athens*, published in London between 1762 and 1814.

'Urn with facets' potpourri vase
Soft-paste porcelain, polychrome decoration
with gold heightening
Sèvres royal manufactory, 1759

'Pygmalion and Galatea'
Etienne-Maurice Falconet, sculptor
Soft-paste biscuit porcelain
Sèvres royal manufactory, 1763

Drop-front writing desk
Philippe-Claude Montigny
Oak, rosewood and amaranth veneer,
chased and gilt bronze, red marble
Paris, c.1765–70

Marie-Antoinette's vestal virgins

The Greek style had been above all a revolt against the excesses of rococo and had erred in its militancy, but the Etruscan style seems to have been typical of a type of refined, femininely graceful type of decoration, like the panelling executed by the Rousseau brothers for Marie-Antoinette at Fontainebleau and Versailles. They covered their panelling with infinitely delicate arabesques* in which the colourful figures of the Renaissance were replaced by slim-ankled deities, amphorae, smoking incense burners and sphinxes with pointed wings.

Jean-Démosthène Dugourc's clock with vestal virgins  (1788), formerly in the Tuileries Palace, with its bronzes by Pierre-Philippe Thomire and porcelain plaques painted at Sèvres, is emblematic of the queen's taste for toned-down Antiquity ❷❸. The same graceful arabesques dance over a series of large decorative panels  painted on canvas, contemporary to Marie-Antoinette's boudoir at Fontainebleau.

In a display case nearby you can see four terracottas by Philippe-Laurent Roland, studies for bas-reliefs of Muses for this boudoir, which was decorated in 1783.

In the late 1780s and early 1790s, the Etruscan style was more directly inspired by Greek vases with a black ground. A cup and saucer  by Jean-Jacques Lagrenée (Sèvres, 1791) is decorated with palm leaves* and foliation* on a black ground. Around the same time, Dugourc decorated the walls and chairs of an Etruscan-style interior with red figures on the same black ground .

The taste for picturesque ruins ❷❹ developed with the vogue for the trip to Italy and, less frequently, to Greece and the

Clock with vestal virgins
Jean-Démosthène Dugourc, designer
Pierre-Philippe Thomire, bronze founder
Etienne-Simon Boizot, sculptor
Soft-paste porcelain, gilt bronze, black-patinated bronze, deep blue and Spanish brocatelle marble
Sèvres royal manufactory, 1788

Decorative panel
Oil on canvas
Paris, c.1780

Cup and saucer
Jean-Jacques Lagrenée, designer
Dubois and Vaudé, painters
Hard-paste porcelain, gold heightening
Sèvres royal manufactory, 1791

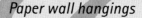

Paper wall hangings

In the early 18th century, English manufacturers had the idea of gluing sheets of paper together end-to-end to make rolls. Wallpaper in the modern sense of the word was born. This technique, adopted in France around 1760, enabled the reproduction of large motifs and the use of rolls revolutionised printing techniques. The engraver's and printer's screw press was abandoned for woodblock printing. The roll was laid on a long wooden table covered with woollen cloth. The carved woodblock was dipped in a tray of colour, placed on the paper and tapped with a mallet or pressed using a lever mechanism powered by weights.

A separate block was used for each colour. The use of distemper, a mixture of pigments, chalk and glue, produced rich matt colours.

In Paris in the 1780s, wallpaper became so fashionable that estate agent's advertisements listed the wallpaper in apartments.

'Autumn'
Length of wallpaper with arabesques
Attributed to Pierre Cietti, designer
Velum paper joined end-to-end, brushed matt white ground,
woodblock printed in 10 colours including gold, brushwork
Réveillon manufactory
Paris, 1786

Design for an interior decoration
Jean-Démosthène Dugourc
Watercolour, pen and black ink, gouache
*C.*1790

Near East. False ruins and antique-style follies sprung up in parks now laid out in the English manner. The painter Hubert Robert designed the tomb of Jean-Jacques Rousseau in the form of an antique cenotaph for the park of the Marquis of Girardin at Ermenonville. The 'painter of ruins' par excellence, Hubert Robert painted six large decorative pictures around 1791 ◉, in which palace terraces and cypress trees reaching to the sky evoke Rome and Tivoli, while other 'Gothic' buildings evoke an 'antiquity' closer to home.

Cabinetmakers produced ingenious folding furniture, combining polished steel, bronze, mahogany and rosewood. The table with parasol ◉ by Martin-Guillaume Biennais (c.1810) still has its original taffetas. Writing desks, overnight cases ◉ and even a watercolour box are testaments to this new cosmopolitan, mobile society. 'Travel souvenirs' began to be produced for these cultivated tourists: small Italian, antique-style bronzes, famous monuments reproduced in faience and porcelain, such as the *Mausoleum of Maria Magdalena Langhans* ◉, in the canton of Berne, by Johan August Nahl, produced in terracotta and in biscuit* by the Nyon manufactory in Switzerland but also by the Niderviller manufactory in Lorraine around 1775. Maria Magdalena Langhans, who died during childbirth, is portrayed breaking open the lid of her tomb—a vision that could have come straight out of a 'Gothic' tale by Horace Walpole or Matthew Lewis.

The rise of mahogany

Mahogany* began to be widely used in cabinetmaking under Louis XVI ㉖. Used as ballast in ships, it was unloaded in major ports such as Bordeaux and Nantes and used there by furniture makers. The enormous wardrobe with two doors and two corner cupboards, simply sculpted with mouldings (Bordeaux, mid-18th century) has the two prime characteristics of French port furniture: elegance and solidity. Despite the resistance of the Parisian cabinetmakers, mahogany finally gained favour in the capital, helped by the love of all things English in the second half of the 18th century. Its technical characteristics, strength and resistance to rot made it the perfect wood for dining rooms and bathrooms.

A cooling table attributed to Canabas sums up these two, far from contradictory influences. A chest of drawers by Leleu, a writing table and a roll-top desk by Riesener, a chest of drawers with doors by Stöckel, a chair with an openwork back ◉ by Georges Jacob (c.1780–90) show the uses the great Parisian cabinetmakers later made of this wood and the wide variety of mahoganies employed: flamed, figured*, burred*, etc. Sober structure, a deliberately restrained use of gilt* bronze, and the absence of marquetry and inlay, give pride of place to the wood itself.

The Gohin Family ◉ by Louis-Léopold Boilly (1787), shows an opulent interior at the end of the Ancien Régime, with its mahogany furniture and extremely sober decoration. The colour merchant Nicolas Gohin, portrayed seated in front of his roll-top desk, invented Prussian blue. His daughter Benjamine is shown with her husband, Henry Jean Baptiste Bouquillard, who had made his fortune in the French

'Mausoleum of Maria Magdalena Langhans'
After the original by Johann August Nahl, 1751
Hard-paste biscuit porcelain
Niderviller manufactory, c.1780–90

Imaginary landscape
Hubert Robert
Oil on canvas
Paris, c.1791

'The Gohin Family'
Louis-Léopold Boilly
Oil on canvas
Paris, 1787

Parasol–table
Martin-Guillaume Biennais
Amaranth, gilt bronze, iron,
steel, taffetas
Paris, c.1810

Breakfast service
Hard-paste porcelain, underglaze
polychrome decoration with gold
heightening; morocco leather-covered case
Meissen manufactory, c.1780–90

Chair with 'flower spray' back
Georges Jacob
Sculpted mahogany and beech,
leather
Paris, c.1780–90

West Indies. The ship he is pointing at is an allusion to his prosperous overseas trade. Shipbuilding attained a high degree of perfection in France under Louis XVI and the scientists of the time were quick to exploit this technical superiority. In 1785, the king sent La Pérouse to explore the North Pacific in the wake of the Bougainville expedition in 1766–69.

Jean Pillement painted his series of *Views of the Benfica Gardens* ● in Lisbon, one of Europe's major trading ports, in 1785. The wood importer Jean Devismes' *quinta* has a magnificent garden with ornamental shrubbery, fountains and statues.

The metamorphoses of the chair

The Chair Gallery ㉕ traces the chair's morphological evolution over a period of over a century. The legs of the imposing, wide-seated chairs of the end of Louis XIV's reign had cross-struts. The bases, cross-struts and armrests of Régence chairs were more sinuous and the S-curved leg was superseded by tauter curves. Around 1740, the cross-strut disappeared. Chairs also became lighter: the back became lower and the wood frame was left visible around the back and seat. Cabriolet chairs, easily movable to facilitate conversation, had a curved back and armrest supports set back on the sides and no longer at the front. The *à la reine* chair had a flat back and shortened armrests to make room for the voluminous dresses with panniers women then wore. In the late 1760s, the Greek style put an end to the flowing curves of rococo. Around 1780, armrests were again aligned with the back legs. The role of the sculptor was eclipsed by that of the turner, whose skills had fallen into disuse in the late 17th

century. The legs were now turned into fluted columns and the armrest supports baluster-shaped.

Porcelain, silver and bronze

In the 18th century, French manufactories attained supreme mastery in the use of a new material, soft-paste porcelain ●, creating innovative forms for decorative and domestic uses. A display case presents examples on a rotary basis, arranged by type and manufactory ㉗.

Pieces from the museum's exceptional silverware collection ● are also displayed on a rotary basis to show the quality of the work of Parisian and provincial silversmiths and several original personalities, and the variety of forms and decorative motifs.

A glass cabinet is devoted to gilt* bronze, the Parisian material par excellence in the 18th century. One of the unusual objects on view is a sumptuous *dévidoir* like the one used by Madame de Pompadour, at whose court ladies did not consider themselves above spinning wool and silk.

Two drawing rooms

The panelling of the Talairac and Serres drawing rooms, bequeathed to the museum in 1919 and 1938 respectively, have enabled us to recreate the atmosphere of two almost contemporary 18th-century décors. The first (c.1790) comes from the Hôtel de Talairac ● (p. 88-89) in rue Neuve-des-Capucins (now rue Joubert), a street created in 1780 ㉘. Its recent restoration revealed the quality of its painted decoration: antique-style foliation imitating bronze, trompe-l'œil

'A la reine' armchair
Sculpted walnut
Paris, c.1720-30

'View of the Benfica Gardens'
Jean Pillement
Oil on canvas
Lisbon, 1785

Cabriolet chair
Louis Delanois
Moulded beech, embossed velvet
Paris, c.1765

Ewer and basin
Robert-Joseph Auguste
Silver-gilt
Paris, 1784–85

'Vine' terrine and 'ornament' dish
Soft-paste porcelain
Vincennes manufactory, c.1752

Chair
Georges Jacob
Painted and sculpted beech, embossed velvet
Paris, c.1770

p. 88-89
Panelling of the drawing room
of the Hôtel de Talairac
Painted and gilt oak and pine
Paris, c.1790

bas-reliefs depicting delicate biscuit porcelain with coloured grounds, and palm leaves and griffons on the wood-grained doors. The red marble and gilt* bronze fireplace, dating from a little later, is a fine illustration of the Egyptian style then emerging. The mahogany furniture, the *en cabinet* writing desk by Stöckel and longcase pendulum clock by Antide Janvier are complemented by an exceptional astronomical clock ◉ (c.1794) by Philippe-Jacques Corniquet, one of whose dials has the ten-hour day imposed by the Republican authorities. The walls are hung with landscapes by Hubert Robert and Claude-Louis Châtelet and history paintings typical of the collection of an art lover at the end of the century of the Enlightenment.

The second drawing room, donated to the museum by the interior designer Eugène Barriol in 1938, was in the Hôtel de Serres ◉ (p. 92–93) in place Vendôme **29**.

More classical in inspiration, it has extremely original and graceful columns reminiscent of the frescoes at Pompeii, and antique-style bas-relief overdoors. A rare detail: the piers of the mirrors descend to the floor, and the mirror is protected by a low balustrade. The drawing room originally had mahogany wall clocks decorated with the same bronze chimeras ◉ as the fireplace ◉, and grey-painted wooden chairs matching the delicate lilac and blue panelling and woodgraining. It is now furnished with giltwood* chairs made around 1780, some of which are by Georges Jacob and Jean-Baptiste-Claude Séné, and several fine veneered pieces by Roger Vandercruse Lacroix.

Astronomical clock
Philippe-Jacques Corniquet
Gilt bronze, enamel face
Paris, c.1794

Fireplace of the drawing room of the Hôtel de Serres
(detail, see p. 92–93)
Blue marble, patinated and gilt bronze
Paris, between 1790 and 1801

Clock: 'Juno on her chariot drawn by peacocks'
Louis-Michel Harel, clockmaker
Chased and gilt bronze, green antique marble, Paris, c.1800

Pair of athéniennes with pineapples
Gilt and blued bronze
Paris, c.1780

Chimera (detail of the fireplace of the drawing room of the Hôtel de Serres)
Patinated and gilt bronze

p. 92–93
Drawing room of the Hôtel de Serres
Attributed to Chérubin Lecomte, architect
Paris, between 1790 and 1801

19th century

By over-throwing the feudal regime and abolishing the privileged orders, the French Revolution marked the advent of a wealthy middle class and the birth of a capitalist economy. The disappearance of the guilds which controlled the production of craftsmen and the creation of the Conservatoire des Arts et Métiers (National School of Arts and Crafts) encouraged the growth of the industrial arts. But the dissolution of the Académie Royale de Peinture et de Sculpture did not lessen the gulf between the decorative and so-called 'fine' arts. The Institut de France, created in 1795 and invested with greater powers by the First Consul in 1803, dominated art education throughout the 19th century through the Académie des Beaux-Arts.

The Empire put the finishing touches to France's unity and consolidated the Revolution's principle social achievements. The international embargo on imports of British goods favoured French industrial progress. The exact sciences made dazzling advances with the discoveries of Ampère, Carnot, Chaptal, Gay-Lussac and Chevreul. During the July Monarchy (1830–48), the growth of industrial capitalism gradually led to the development of the working class. Nurtured by revolutionary upheavals and the drawn-out Napoleonic Wars, a morbid sensibility pervaded literary and artistic creation from the 1820s to the 1840s: Romanticism was born.

The political stability of the Second Empire (1852–70) ushered in a period of great prosperity. The first department stores opened, the railway network developed, the Suez Canal was completed and, motivated by positivist ideals, Emile Littré and Pierre Larousse published their dictionaries. In 1863, the Salon des Refusés, where Manet's work caused a uproar, sealed the artistic avant-garde's divorce with the academic system. The leader of the Naturalist school, Emile Zola, painted a vast social panorama in his novels. France's defeat in 1870 by Prussia and the loss of Alsace-Lorraine prompted the birth of the nationalist movement.

'Winter Garden'
(detail, see p. 111)

1801

The invention of the Jacquard loom simplifies the weaving of the most complex fabrics.

1850

Joseph Paxton designs the first large metal and glass building, the Crystal Palace, in the London suburbs.

1874

The first exhibition of the Impressionnists in Paris.

1882

Primary education becomes compulsory in France.

19th century

The Revolution profoundly changed mentalities. Political debates tore the nation apart, blood was shed, artists received fewer and fewer commissions and light-hearted ornamentation disappeared overnight. In the 1790s, the straight line and Antiquity were more than ever the order of the day and culminated in the solemn, austere and sumptuous art of the Empire.

But Antiquity was no longer regarded in the same way. The new style pioneered by David matched the spirit of the time: his simplicity, heroic drapery and taste for the motto sealed the rift between the taste of the Ancien Régime and the fledgling democracy. Via a process of gradual simplification, the new, rigorous classicism eclipsed the grace of the closing century. Mahogany, flamed, flecked or figured, was still the cabinet-making wood par excellence, but marquetry disappeared. The most expensive furniture was now inlaid with wood or metal. Violent colour contrasts between woods—between black ebony and pale yellow lemonwood, for instance—became increasingly popular.

Yet in 1791 the Le Chapelier Law abolished the guilds and the Revolutionary authorities reorganised the furniture crafts. From then on the joiner tolerated the cabinetmaker and vice versa. A single workshop could now employ cabinet-makers, bronze founders and gilders and produce every component of a piece of furniture itself. It was no longer obligatory to stamp* a piece of furniture, although most of the greatest cabinetmakers continued to do so.

The furniture made during the Directoire and Consulat, paid lip service to the new rigour but never abandoned a certain graceful elegance. The back of the curule chair ☙, whose refined design enables its attribution to the cabinetmaker Jacob, is decorated with an antique tripod. Its straight, 'Etruscan style' back legs, a feature which first appeared during

Louis XVI's reign, are attached to the seat rim with a volute imitating the fastenings on Roman chairs. Three new pieces of furniture appeared in the late 18th century. The *athénienne*, directly inspired by the Greek tripod, could be used as a washbasin, as a flower pot or, like the small bronze example ☙ by Jean-Baptiste-Claude Odiot (1763–1850), as an incense burner. Another newcomer was the *psyché*, a large vertically pivot-able mirror. Elegant men and women could now see themselves from head to foot while dressing—a revolution made possible by the production of ever larger, but still extremely costly mirrors. But the psyché was soon dethroned by the mirrored wardrobe, which appeared during the July Monarchy.

The boat bed, on the other hand, remained popular throughout the century. In 1828, the designer Santi wrote in his introduction to his *Models for Furniture* [...]: 'The idea for the form of these came from a boat rocking languidly on the waves.'

David and the pomp of Empire

After masterminding the great processions of the Revolution, the painter Jacques-Louis David (1748–1825) went on to direct the pomp of Napoleon's Empire ③⓪. Apart from the influence of his studio, where several generations of artists trained, he left his mark on fashion, furniture and even the theatre, advising Talma. As early as 1784, David designed his own antique-style furniture, which he had

Athénienne incense burner
Jean-Baptiste-Claude Odiot
Patinated bronze
Paris, 1819

Curule chair
Attributed to Jacob Frères
Mahogany
Paris, Directoire 1795–99

'Paris and Helen'
Jacques-Louis David
Oil on canvas
Paris, 1789

made by Jacob, and depicted several of these pieces in his pictures.

Paris and Helen ● (p. 97), dated 1789, is a curious mixture of this reinvented Antiquity and Jean Goujon's *Caryatids* in the Louvre, in the background, which were sculpted during the Renaissance. His representation of the human body now obeyed the precepts of the *Beau idéal* (ideal beauty), which sought to correct nature using the canons of that infallible paragon of absolute beauty, Greco-Roman sculpture.

Two other personalities dominated the decorative arts: the architects Charles Percier (1764–1838) and Pierre-François Léonard Fontaine (1762–1853). Both worked for Jacob then Joséphine, the First Consul's wife, who had them transform the Château de Malmaison. For the Emperor, they restored and decorated the Tuileries Palace, the Louvre, Saint-Cloud, Compiègne, Fontainebleau and Rambouillet. They were for Napoleon what Lebrun was for Louis XIV, the guarantors of the reign's stylistic unity. The museum has a rare copy of the 1812 edition of their highly influential *Album of Interior Decorations* (1801), watercoloured by the painter Benjamin Gotthold, Count of Schlick (1796–1872), during the Restauration ●.

Their creed? To disseminate the principles of taste taught by Antiquity, combining them, in their own words, with 'those general laws of the simple, true and beautiful' in rigorously symmetrical compositions. In 1756, in his *Reflections on the Imitation of Greek Works in Painting and Sculpture*, the German archaeologist Winckelmann, one of the most passionate proponents of Greek beauty, declared: 'Good taste, which is spreading more and more in the world, began to take form under Greek skies. [...] The only means for us to become great and, if possible, inimitable, is to imitate the Ancients [...].'

In 1808, Napoleon preached much the same thing, but with other ambitions: 'I have set my heart on seeing French artists efface the glory of Athens and Italy.' To help them in this, the Muséum Central des Arts, founded by the Convention and renamed the Musée Napoléon (the present-day Louvre) was enriched with the fabulous booty of his military campaigns, and notably with the most famous antiquities from the Italian collections.

Greek and Roman mythology left the museums and invaded furniture. The total disappearance of marquetry, now regarded as outmoded, cleared the way for ornamental bronzes to gleam on large surfaces of polished mahogany*. Their gilding* was either brilliant or, more frequently, matt, their chasing precise and the perfection of their design and execution sometimes rather cold. The repertoire of these decorative bronzes was almost infinite, ranging from martial attributes such as the sword and helmet to sinuous figures with butterfly's wings, the Labours of Hercules, Apollo's and Venus' chariots, griffons and languid swans ❸❸.

From Egypt to Rome

Ornamentalists mixed Egyptian motifs, known from certain monuments in Rome, with classical Antiquity to create an exotic new repertoire, and General Bonaparte's Egyptian campaign in 1798 encouraged this vogue. The base of an escritoire by Lemarchand (c.1805), the muzzles of whose lions have the pharoah's *nemes* beard, show the freedom with which this vocabulary was exploited during the Empire.

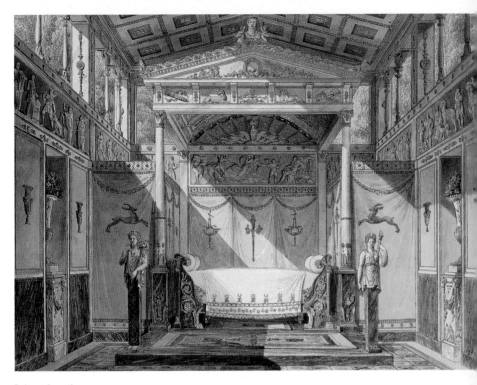

Bedroom decoration
Charles Percier, Pierre-François Léonard Fontaine, engravings
Benjamin Gotthold, Count of Schlick, watercolouring
Watercoloured engravings
Paris, c.1825

**Fireplace of the Large Study
in the Tuileries Palace**
Charles Percier,
Pierre-François Léonard Fontaine,
engravings
Benjamin Gotthold, Count of Schlick,
watercolouring
Watercoloured engravings
Paris, c.1825

Stylised caryatid columns, with their bronze heads and feet and rigid mahogany bodies, distant offspring of the Roman herms*, are just as whimsical. Around the keyholes, tamed lions and sheep on leashes are being led to sacrifice.

Paper décors

Wallpaper, whose production became increasingly sophisticated, remained unwaveringly popular throughout the century. The first scenic wallpapers were created, and walls could now 'open' onto architectural vistas or landscapes peopled with historic or exotic figures. One of the most famous scenic wallpapers produced early in the century was the *Story of Psyche* ◉, designed by Louis Laffitte and Méry-Joseph Blondel and produced by the Dufour company (1814). Its Davidian figures are set in a décor worthy of Percier and Fontaine, with antique-style furniture copied from Jacob. Although the *Story of Psyche* was printed in grisaille*, twenty-three colours were used. Spectacular wallpapers such as this had the advantage of being infinitely less costly than a traditional décor of painted panelling, yet they were still affordable only by the wealthy.

A bronze Olympus

Interior decoration's accessories also had to fulfil the dual exigency of rigor and sumptuousness ❸. Gilt* candelabra ◉ were held up by black-patinated bronze gods and goddesses, winged victories and antique spirits standing on altar-like plinths. Bearded herms* supported oil lamps called 'quinquets' after their supposed inventor. Crystal was engraved with bas-relief* figures evoking glyptics*. The delicately draped figures of the goddess Athena and the nine Muses grace the sides of a crystal ewer ◉ attributed to the Montcenis manufactory. A sumptuous display of gilt or silvered bronze cooling buckets, soup tureens, dishes, vases and ewers by Jean-Baptiste-Claude Odiot ◉, one of the greatest precious metalsmiths of the first half of the 19th century, are peopled with delightful flowing figures. The perfection of the chasing makes their very dense foliation and palm and vine leaf decoration sparkle. Odiot perfected a very simple technique for obtaining a perfect contrast between polished surfaces and ornaments: the latter were worked separately then fixed to the object with screws. Concerned by his posterity, he donated his bronze models to the state, and they were subsequently silver-plated by the Christofle manufactory.

Odiot also made the cup with the form of a breast ◉, moulded from Pauline Bonaparte, Napoleon's sister and wife of Prince Camillo Borghese. This beauty famous for her loose morals was immortalised in marble by Canova. The cup's butterfly handle evokes the legend of Psyche and female fickleness.

Honey-coloured wood

In 1815, as the restored monarchy was taking up residence in Napoleon's apartments, joiners and cabinetmakers continued to produce Empire furniture ❸. At the outset, they merely did away with the emblems of the previous reign—bees, eagles, thunderbolts and the attributes of the warrior—replacing them with more innocuous insignia such as garlands,

'Story of Psyche: Psyche Intending to Stab the Sleeping Cupid'
Scenic wallpaper
Joseph Dufour manufactory, 1815
Republished by the Desfossé & Karth manufactory
Mechanical paper, painted grey ground
1872

'Mars'
Candelabrum
Patinated bronze, gilt bronze
France, First Empire (1804–14)

'Athena and the Nine Muses' ewer and basin
Attributed to the Montcenis manufactory
Blown, carved and wheel-engraved crystal
France, First Empire (1804–14)

Cup with the form of Pauline Borghese's breast
Jean-Baptiste-Claude Odiot
Gilt bronze
Paris, c.1810

Cooling bucket
Jean-Baptiste-Claude Odiot
Silver plated bronze
Paris, 1819–23

bunches of roses and dolphins. Antique references became less marked. The rediscovery of France's indigenous, often light-coloured woods, wrongly attributed to the reign of Charles X, in fact dates back to the continental blockade against England begun in 1806. Ash, plane, maple and elm became extremely fashionable during the Restauration. Burred* wood was highly prized for the richness of its meandering veins, as was speckled burr wood.

The Duchess of Berry, daughter of the King of Naples and Charles X's daughter-in-law, was the figurehead of this new fashion. The impish princess shook up the starchy etiquette at court in the Tuileries Palace. In 1823, she redecorated her apartment in the Marsan pavilion in the Louvre, several of whose rooms are now part of the Musée des Arts Décoratifs. Her bedroom is evoked by the two pieces of furniture by Félix Rémond she bought at the Exhibition of Products of Industry in 1827. The burred* elm, ash and walnut-veneered *psyché* ◉ plays on the contrasts between these light-coloured woods and the subtle inlaid decoration. The base contains a six-tune music box with 24 pipes that was greatly admired in 1823. The profusion of appliqué bronzes on the queen's burred elm and amboine-veneered dressing table is reminiscent of certain Empire pieces.

The Duchess of Berry's psyché with music box
Félix Rémond, cabinetmaker
Oak, burred elm, ash and walnut veneer, gilt bronze
Paris, 1823

The miracle child

Seven months after her husband's assassination in 1820, the Duchess of Berry gave birth to a son, the Duke of Bordeaux and future Count of Chambord. The cradle of this 'miracle child' was made by Félix Rémond ◉. It was veneered with burred*

Ceremonial cradle of the Duke of Bordeaux
Félix Rémond, cabinetmaker
Denière and Matelin, bronze founders
Oak, burred ash, elm, walnut and amaranth veneer, gilt bronze
Paris, 1819

The bourgeois bedroom

From the 1840s, the evolution of the bedroom was influenced by two new factors: the desire for a healthier environment and the advent of the marriage bed. The exigencies of greater hygiene led to the simplification of the drapery surrounding the bed. Woollen fabrics, which harboured dust, were replaced by cotton and silk. The use of sprung mattresses spread.

At the Château d'Eu and the Tuileries Palace, King Louis-Philippe and his wife now shared the same bedroom. The bed grew larger, like English beds. Bedside tables began to be made in pairs and this tendency was adopted by the bourgeoisie. Bedroom furniture also included a chest of drawers, a mirrored wardrobe (which dethroned the psyché*), a dressing table with a marble top and comfortable chairs. Only very luxuriously-appointed apartments had a separate water closet. The bathroom did not become a common feature until after the turn of the century.

Blue room
Léger
Watercolour
France, 1844

elm, figured* ash, inlaid with amaranth and decorated with gilt* bronzes. Its allegories and symbols were carefully chosen. Renown is holding up a horn of plenty overflowing with France's riches to the heavens: fruit, vegetables and fleur-de-lis, emblem of the French monarchy. The heir to the throne's 'boat' symbolises the regime's political stability after the turmoil of the Napoleonic era. Medallions depicting the sciences and the arts illustrate the benefits of this newfound prosperity.

The large Sèvres vase with gold and platinum fleur-de-lis on a blue ground, dated 1820, commemorates the Duke of Bordeaux's birth ◉. The medallion, painted by Alexandre-Evariste Fragonard following instructions by Théodore Brongniart, director of the Sèvres manufactory, shows the royal child assembling a *jeu d'onchet* symbolising society's various classes – a difficult task which the prince, who never became king, would never have to undertake.

The boat bed by François Baudry ◉, a masterpiece of cabinetmaking veneered with ash and elm and inlaid with amaranth, won a prize at the Exhibition of Products of Industry in 1827. There is not a single straight line in its ship-like structure.

The lightness of the wood stands out against a famous scenic wallpaper by the Dufour & Leroy manufactory, *Renaldo and Armida* ◉. The scenes depicted, from Tasso's famous epic poem, *Jerusalem Delivered*, were merely a pretext to show luxuriant landscapes peopled with small figures in historic costume. It is noteworthy in this respect that it is listed in Dufour & Leroy's registers as a 'coloured landscape'. These scenic wallpapers were woodblock printed except for their coloured grounds, which were hand-painted as this was the only means of obtaining subtly-gradated tones.

The display cases contain a unique collection of objects in opaline, whose translucent 'soap bubble', pigeon-throat pink and opaque turquoise colours created an original harmony with the light-coloured woods. *The pair of Medici vases* ◉ (p. 109), a technical tour-de-force, are particularly rare.

In the home of a man of taste

This exquisite palette would have been out of place in the sumptuous apartment the Anglo-Dutch banker William Hope decorated from 1838 in the former Hôtel de Monaco in rue Saint-Dominique. His bedroom ◉ (p. 106–07) is a very free interpretation of French Renaissance motifs with violently contrasting blues, reds, greens and abundant gilding ㉟.

The ebony-veneered chest of drawers-cum-writing desk by Alexandre-Louis Bellangé, son and nephew of a line of cabinetmakers going back to the late 18th century, was inspired by the compartmentalised decoration of 17th-century cabinets. As in the transitional furniture at the end of the Ancien Régime, the writing table is concealed behind false drawers. The bronze bed, painted to imitate wood and highly representative of the Neo-Renaissance style in the 1840s, is not the original bed.

Boat bed
François Baudry
Grey poplar, burred and figured ash, burred elm, amaranth,
Santo-Domingan lemonwood and mahogany veneer
France, 1827

Vase commemorating the birth of the Duke of Bordeaux
Hard-paste porcelain, polychrome, gold and bronze decoration
Sèvres manufactory, 1820

**'Renaldo and Armida or Jerusalem Delivered:
Clorinda's Tomb and the Crusaders' Camp'**
Scenic wallpaper
Leroy & Dufour manufactory
Woodblock-printed, hand-painted grounds
Paris, 1830–31

p. 106–07
Baron William Hope's bedroom
Sculpted, painted and gilt panelling,
stucco decoration
Paris, 1838–40

19th century

The past refound

Louis-Philippe's reign was infused with that integral component of Romanticism, nostalgia for the art of the past and especially the Gothic era, introduced by the Duchess of Berry around 1820. The 'king-citizen' endeavoured to unite the nation around its heroic past not the ideals of Antiquity. He set the example himself at the Château de Pau and in his favourite residence, the Château d'Eu, which he had refurnished in the medieval and 17th-century style yet with all the luxury of his own time. The room evoking the craze for curios **36** contains one of the most famous objects of this historicist* movement, the bronze version of the *Renaissance Vase* 👁 by Claude-Aimé Chenavard (1798-1838). The albums of ornaments of this prolific artist and writer exercised considerable influence over the industrial arts. His main sources of inspiration were the Middle Ages and the Renaissance, and he produced numerous designs for the Sèvres manufactory. There is also porcelain by Jacob Petit and various 'Gilbert and Sullivan Gothic' objects. The extraordinary bouquet of flowers magnified inside the solid crystal paper weight 👁, made at the Clichy manufactory and inspired by the Italian *millefiori*, is composed of minute sticks of glass.

A waltz of flowers

The ebony* and blackened pearwood furniture so popular during Louis-Philippe's reign encountered an unexpected competitor in the 1840s **37**. Black wood and papier-mâché furniture and objects began to be made, inlaid with mother-of-pearl* and painted with brightly-coloured flowers

'Bouquet dressé' paper weight
Crystal lined with 'Pompadour pink', carved, inclusions of mosaic rods
Clichy manufactory, 1845–55

Vase
Claude-Aimé Chenavard
Patinated bronze and coloured stones
France, c.1830

108

Opaline

In the late 18th century, French manufacturers succeeded in imitating the renowned brilliance of English crystal*. During the Empire, the colouring of crystal glass led to what is now known as opaline but was then called crystal opal or opal-coloured crystal. Luxury opaline objects—bowls, ring boxes, vases and mantelpiece decorations—initially had the simple forms of the return to Antiquity and often gilt* bronze mounts. But forms became fuller under Charles X and even more curved during the Second Empire. Colours, inspired by Bohemian vases, became brighter. Delicate pinks were obtained using gold salts. From 1840, to economise on gold, pink glass was no longer tinted all the way through but lined with coloured glass. In the early 19th century, Le Creusot, Baccarat and Saint-Louis were the main production centres. Later, crystal factories sprung up around Paris at Bercy, Choisy-le-Roi, Belleville and Clichy.

Sugar bowl or fruit dish with dolphins
Opal crystal, carved cabling, gilt bronze mount
France, c.1820

Pair of Medici vases
Blown bicolour opal crystal, chased and gilt bronze
Bercy manufactory?, 1815–30

heightened with gold ☜. This type of furniture, which originated in Victorian England, emerged with the increasing industrialisation of furniture production. It was still decorated by hand, which gave these cheaply-produced pieces an illusion of luxury. Flowers also invaded furnishing fabrics and wallpaper.

One of the most famous Second Empire wallpapers, *Winter Garden* ☜, designed by Edouard Müller (1823–76) and produced by Jules Desfossé's Parisian manufactory, depicts a fantastic garden. Presented at the 1855 Universal Exhibition, Müller and Desfossé's composition required 381 colours and 360 different woodblocks to print. It depicts a huge glass conservatory, reminiscent of the Crystal Palace which housed the International Exhibition in London in 1851, and echoes the contemporary vogue for winter gardens. These conservatories had become a feature of luxury residences.

The winter garden of Princess Mathilde (1820–1904), the Emperor's cousin, in rue de Courcelles ☜ was the most famous. Her 'veranda', like a clearing in a jungle, was furnished with marble busts of the imperial family. The Goncourt brothers recounted the 'good princess's' passion for flowers: '31 December [1862]. There we were in the round drawing room. There was nobody but an enormous bouquet, as big as the pedestal which it entirely covers, all white camellias and roses and bordered with small blue flowerets with the princess's monogram, *M*, in red flowers in the middle.'

The Universal Exhibitions

The Universal Exhibitions were the successors of the Exhibitions of Products of Industry which Napoleon instituted to stimulate the French economy. Fuelled by Franco-British rivalry, they became extraordinary showcases for the 'industrial arts', as they were then called, and encouraged competition between the great European workshops and manufactories. They were held in London in 1851 and 1862, in Paris in 1855, 1867, 1878, 1889 and 1900, in Vienna in 1873, Amsterdam in 1883 and Chicago in 1893. Concerned that their work should be recognised as 'artistic', the most famous Parisian cabinetmakers of the time vied with one another in the production of 'masterpieces' for these exhibitions ❸. The sculpted walnut cabinet ☜ Henri-Auguste Fourdinois presented at the 1867 Exhibition, freely inspired by Renaissance two-piece wardrobes, is a mixture of extremely architectural structure and a bevy of dazzlingly virtuoso sculptures. It is inlaid with red jasper and lapis lazuli and inside with ivory and silver. Henri was the son of Alexandre-Georges Fourdinois, who founded the family firm in 1835. The Fourdinois company made furniture for the Crown and wealthy clients such as the bankers Pereire and Hottinguer, and reached its peak during the Second Empire. As well as prestigious commissions for the Saint-Cloud and Tuileries palaces, the imperial yacht and pieces for the Universal Exhibitions, its workshops also produced furniture for the ministries and also less costly, simple, solid yet elegant pieces.

'Winter Garden'
Scenic wallpaper
Jules Desfossé manufactory
Edouard Müller, designer
Mechanical paper,
hand-painted background,
woodblock-printed, 381 colours
France, 1853

'Princess Mathilde's Veranda'
Sébastien-Charles Giraud
Oil on wood
Paris, 1864

Gondola chair
Lacquered wood, papier-mâché,
mother-of-pearl inlay, gilding, caning
France, c.1850–65

Two-piece cabinet
Henri-Auguste Fourdinois
Sculpted walnut, red jasper and lapis lazuli inlay
Paris, 1867

The eroticisation of decoration

The cabinet the architect Pierre Manguin designed for the 1855 Universal Exhibition was more faithful to the form of its French Renaissance models, but was decorated with a profusion of gilt* bronzes completely alien to the reign of the Valois kings. It delighted one of the most fashionable demi-monde personalities of the time, Thérèse Lachmann, Marchioness of Païva, who asked Manguin to design her a mansion on the Champs-Elysées. The Hôtel de Païva, built in the Neo-Renaissance style, became a kind of laboratory for the sculptors Carrier-Belleuse, Jules Dalou ◉ and Auguste Rodin, and the painter Paul Baudry. Manguin supervised every detail of the mansion's interior decoration.

Apart from their joint espousal of the Renaissance style, Manguin's and Fourdinois' prestigious cabinets also reflected an incontestable 'eroticisation' of decoration. This was also symptomatic of the beginnings of a kind of star system amongst artisans. They now sought fame at the Universal Exhibitions with pieces that had to be striking, alluring and of course win the gold medal in their discipline. In parallel, at the annual Salons that were a focal point of artistic life during the Second Empire, every subject was now a pretext to paint or sculpt the female nude. The public were not in the slightest bit shocked by this, on the contrary—as long as the academic canons of beauty were respected.

Silvered metal

The *Cent Couverts* centrepiece ◉ set was commissioned for the imperial dining table by Prince-President Louis Napoleon Bonaparte, the future Napoleon III, in 1852. Made by the Christofle manufactory and finished in 1856, it is both extremely classical in style and daring in execution—it was made in galvanic bronze* and sliver-plated using an electrolytic* process. The pieces presented here were damaged in the fire which gutted the Tuileries Palace in 1871 but they miraculously survived.

Japan in Paris

The gradual opening up of Japan to international trade and the massive importing of objects from the Far East sowed the seeds for an artistic revolution which reached its peak in the 1880s. At the International Exhibition in London in 1862, visitors were fascinated by over 600 objects brought back from Japan by two British diplomats. This fascination continued at the Universal Exhibition in Paris in 1867, where, for the first time, Japan came and presented its art itself.

The corner cabinet ◉ designed by the architect and ornamentalist Emile Reiber (1826–93), who worked for the Christofle company, makes fanciful use of various decorative elements inspired by Japanese pieces from the contemporary Meiji era. The central metal relief panel was oxidised using a complex process perfected by Christofle around that time. The cabinet was shown at the Universal Exhibition in 1878, where Christofle showed pieces in the Japanese style. It perfectly illustrates the contradictions of the Japonist movement, torn between the picturesque and a yearning for geometric stylisation.

Corner cabinet
Christofle & Cie
Grohé Frères, cabinetmaker
Emile Reiber, designer
Ebony, rosewood, blackened pearwood,
gilt and patinated galvanic bronze,
copper, silver, gold, cloisonné enamel
Paris, 1874–78

Console table
Aimé-Jules Dalou,
Albert-Ernest Carrier-Belleuse, sculptors
Patinated bronze, gilt bronze, red marble, onyx, alabaster
Paris, 1864–65

The 'Cent Couverts' centrepiece
Christofle & Cie, manufacturer
Silvered bronze and galvanic bronze
Paris, 1852–56

113

Fauns and centaurs ❸❾

Two large book cabinets in blackened
pearwood by Guéret Frères ◉ and a third
in the Neo-Greek style contain a selection
of rare objects, ranging from the dishes
by Constant Sévin cast by Barbedienne to
the terracotta sketches by Jean-Baptiste
Carpeaux for the monumental figures
decorating the Marsan pavilion...

A display case is devoted to faience in the
style of Bernard Palissy, which Charles-
Jean Avisseau made his speciality. The
precious metalsmith Emile Froment-
Meurice (1837–1937) enlisted the services
of the sculptor Emile-François Carlier for
the extraordinary, partially gilt* cen-
taurs and fauns of his *Centrepiece with
Fritillaries* ◉, whose rock crystal dishes
are surmounted by silver-gilt* fritillaries.
It was shown at the Universal Exhibition
in 1867. The contrast between the naturalist treatment of the plants and the
mythological figures was widely praised.
The version on display here is Froment-
Meurice's studio prototype, which he kept.

'Centrepiece with Fritillaries':
dish and pair of candelabrum
Emile Froment-Meurice, silversmith
Emile-François Carlier, sculptor
Glass, gilt bronze, silvered metal
Paris, 1867

In the 'lionesses' cage

The high-flying courtesans, or 'lionesses',
'cocottes' or 'demi-mondaines', were some
of the most prominent society personalities of the time ❹❶. In 1879, Gustave Doré
(1832–83) designed a monumental gilt*
bronze clock for his mistress, the actress
and *dame galante* Alice Ozi. Pitiless Time,
perched atop the globe, is reaping the
loves which seem to slip over the polished
metal. The beautiful Alice is depicted in
Les Pierrots, Thomas Couture's wallpaper
composition produced by Desfossé. This
evocation of a night of orgy was shown
at the Universal Exhibition in 1867, where

Book cabinet
Guéret Frères
Oak structure, ebony and blackened pear veneer,
mahogany interior
Paris, c.1870

Bad Taste

Every period has its definition of bad taste. During the age of Classicism, medieval art was considered barbarous or 'Gothic'. Stendhal wrote, 'What seemed delightful to the cultivated elite of one century, was considered the height of ridiculousness by the good company which replaced it a hundred years later.' In the 19th century, the acceleration of industrialisation and mass-production directly affected taste.

Factories now produced for modest incomes what had previously been affordable only by an elite—who no longer dictated taste. Machine-sawn marquetry*, mass-moulded objects, substitute materials such as papier-mâché and ebonite, painted fabrics imitating repoussé leather, cast-iron covered with graceful Renaissance foliation and alloys imitating gilt* bronze revolutionised furniture production. In the 1850s, interiors became swamped with curios, and those anxious to combat the perversions of this craze came together to form the movement which culminated in the creation of the Union Centrale des Beaux-Arts Appliqués à l'Industrie, the future Union Centrale des Arts Décoratifs.

In his novel Against Nature (1884), Huysmans' describes an aesthete's desperate struggle against ugliness, and whose most extreme refinement was to collect the real flowers best imitating artificial ones.

Troubadour clock
Gilt, silvered and patinated bronze, glass
Paris, c.1840

Incense burner in the form of a vase
Jacob Petit
Hard-paste porcelain,
polychrome and gold decoration
Paris and Fontainebleau, c.1834–48

Desfossé chose 'The Vices and the Virtues' as the theme of his enormous stand. Dalous' powerful console table supported by two bronze atlases was originally in the Hôtel de Païva. The architect Edouard Lièvre (1829–86) designed the bronze ceremonial bed for Louise Delabigne, the red-haired beauty whose professional name was Valtesse de La Bigne. Both the bed and its owner were immortalised by Zola in his novel *Nana*. This monument to love once stood on a platform, in a room entirely hung with sky-blue silk velvet.

Fantastic animals ㊶

When he arrived in Paris in 1870, the Swiss Eugène Grasset was initially influenced by Viollet-le-Duc and the art of the Middle Ages. Then, a few years later, his discovery of Chinese and Japanese art led to his friendship with Charles Gillot, publisher of *Le Japon artistique*, the review edited by Siegfried Bing, the initiator of Art Nouveau in France. The dining-room furniture Grasset designed for Gillot ◉ (p. 118–19) around 1880 is a curious synthesis of diverse styles and influences: Renaissance architecture, fantastic and Celtic animals and plants drawn from nature. The bases of the chair, with their flying buttress-like lateral reinforcements foreshadowing Art Nouveau, are particularly remarkable. The walls and furniture are covered with ceramics by Théodore Deck, Eugène Rousseau, Albert Dammouse and Félix Braquemond among others. All these artists had a passion for ancient French (Saint-Porchaire), Turkish (Iznik), Hispano-Moorish, Chinese and Japanese ceramics. And all were searching for new forms and the secrets of ancient, forgotten techniques.

Nightmarish visions ㊷

Several years after France's humiliating defeat by Prussia in 1870, a group of writers and artists began forging a new art. Their gods were poets: Baudelaire, Verlaine, Mallarmé, Barbey d'Aurevilly. Although it was a tendency rather than a movement with precise aims, Symbolism was brilliantly summed up by the writer Tristan Corbière: 'One must paint only what one has never seen and never will.' Their phantasmagorical visions oscillating between mysticism and decadence, dream and nightmare, and monsters engendered by the sleep of reason haunted the sculptors Rodin and Carriès ◉. Serpents and dragons straight out of the paintings of Gustave Moreau squirm over the jardinière by Edouard Lièvre ◉ and cling to the disturbing mirror attributed to Gabriel Viardot ◉. And in the design for a fountain by the painter James Tissot ◉, they are threatening to overturn the globe upon which lucid Fortune is balancing.

'Head of a Faun'
Jean Joseph Marie Carriès
Glazed stoneware
Saint-Amand-en-Puisaye, 1890–91

Jardinière
Edouard Lièvre, designer
F. Barbedienne, bronze founder
Chased and patinated bronze
Paris, 1870–80

Wall mirror
Attributed to Gabriel Viardot
Sculpted sycamore, mirror glass
Paris, c.1880

'Fortune'
Design for a fountain
James Tissot
Patinated bronze, silvered bronze, gilt bronze,
cloisonné enamel, silver, glass, walnut
France, 1878–82

Bed of Emilie Valtesse de La Bigne
Edouard Lièvre
Wood, gilt bronze, silk velvet
Paris, c.1875

p. 118–19
Furniture for Charles Gillot
and his daughter Marcelle Seure
Eugène Grasset, designer
Fulgraff, cabinetmaker and sculptor
Paris, c.1879–1905

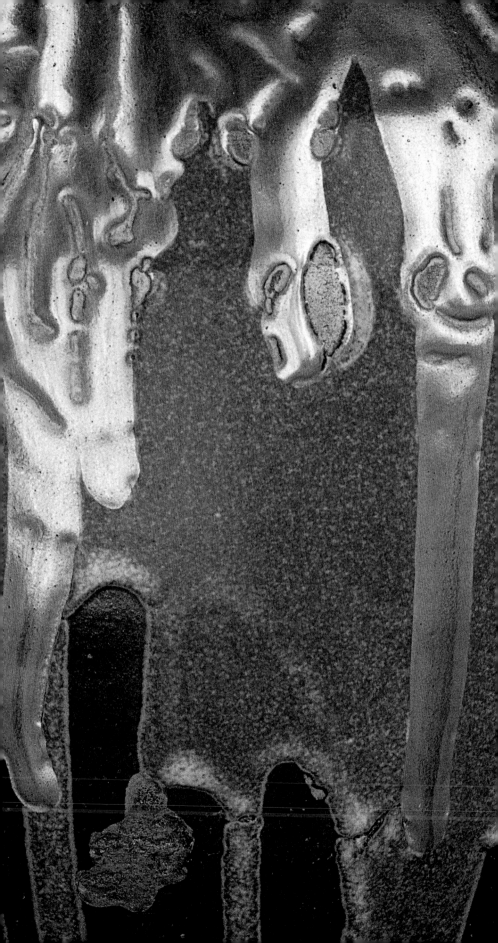

Art Nouveau

In turn authoritarian, opportunist, radical, moderate and anticlerical, the Third Republic was rocked by a series of crises and political scandals: the Decorations and Panama affairs, the Boulangiste crisis, the Dreyfus affair in 1897, and the troubles linked to the law separating Church and State in 1905. The Social unrest generated by the struggle for the eight-hour working day was brutally repressed by Clemenceau, Président du Conseil from 1906 to 1909. France's colonial empire, begun under Charles X, expanded under Napoleon III and Jules Ferry's Republic. In 1914, the French influence spread to North Africa, West Africa, Equatorial Africa, Indochina, Madagascar, the West Indies, Oceania and the trading ports of India.

In Paris, the Universal Exhibitions in 1889 and 1900 were showcases for the triumph of industrial civilisation. Paris inaugurated its underground railway, the Métropolitain. Electricity and the automobile revolutionised lifestyles. Reinforced concrete began to be used in building. In 1894, the engineer Hennebique built the first reinforced concrete bridge in Switzerland. In the Musée d'Ethnographie in the Palais du Trocadéro, avant-garde artists discovered *l'art nègre*. In 1907, Picasso and Braque painted the first Cubist pictures. In 1910, Kandinsky painted his first abstract watercolour.

In a symphonic landscape transformed by Wagner, Paris vied with Vienna for the title of musical capital of Europe. Claude Debussy's *Pelleas and Melisande* was performed for the first time in 1902. Igor Stravinsky's *Rite of Spring*, danced by Diaghilev and his Ballets Russes, caused a scandal in 1913.

1895
The Lumière brothers show films in Paris.

1896
First modern Olympic Games in Athens.

1905
The Fauves create a scandal at the Salon d'Automne.

1909
Louis Blériot flies across the English Channel.

Vase
Jean Joseph Marie Carriès
(detail, see p. 131)

Art Nouveau

In Italy, it was called the *Liberty style*, after the famous store in London, in Spain *Modernismo*, in Germany *Jugendstil* (Young Style), in Austria *Sezessionstil*, after the group of artists who broke with academicism, and there were other names such as the *Modern Style*.

But in France it was called L'Art Nouveau, after the name of the influential gallery Siegfried Bing opened in Paris in 1895. Artists no longer looked to the past for inspiration, convinced that a Gothic cathedral or a Louis XVI cabriolet could no longer serve as models for contemporary creation. Art Nouveau was not a movement but a federation of individuals exploring diverse paths in their quest to revolutionise the living space. The architect and architectural theorist Viollet-le-Duc, whose influence endured until the beginning of the 20th century, notably in Guimard's work, wrote in 1866: 'There is *style*, there are *styles* [...] What is style, then? In a work of art it is the manifestation of an ideal established around a principle [...].' Art Nouveau epitomises this quest for style.

An oasis of clarity

The Universal Exhibition in Paris in 1900 marked the triumph of these new aspirations and, already, the beginning of their decline. In 1900, the Union Centrale des Arts Décoratifs (UCAD) asked the interior designer Georges Hoentschel to design its pavilion. Part of the panelling and furniture of the *Wood Drawing Room* ● (p. 124–25), as it was called, was installed in the new Musée des Arts Décoratifs for its inauguration in 1905. The beautiful honey–coloured Algerian plane wood enhances its plant-inspired sculpted decoration. Hoentschel chose the *Rosa gallica* as its leitmotif to assert the eminent 'Frenchness' of this pavilion in such a cosmopolitan exhibi-

tion, and above all to demarcate it from its Germanic rivals. This French species of hawthorn mingles with laurel on the silk brocade wall fabric. Emile Gallé enthusiastically described the décor as 'an oasis of clarity', writing, '[...] on the wall fabric, on the panelling, there is but one flower to be seen, the dog rose, discreetly singing the poem of youth and spring.' *The Happy Island,* the large painting by Albert Besnard, a brilliant colourist then at the height of his fame, was also commissioned by UCAD. Pictures by Edmond Aman-Jean and a sculpture by Jean Dampt, *Peace in the Home,* in its little olivewood edifice, complete the décor. Two technical and artistic masterpieces were also displayed in this room: the chased and enamelled gold *The Artistic Crafts* goblet ● by Lucien Falize, whose figures were painted by Luc-Olivier Merson (1846–1920), a prominent artist who contributed to the decoration of the Opéra-Comique, and Jules Brateau's (1844-1923) ivory and gold *The Secret* casket ●, enamelled by Paul Grandhomme, a veritable miniature monument. Never had the complicity between the decorative arts and the 'fine' arts attained such complete fusion.

In the small display cases you can see glass by the American Louis Comfort Tiffany (1848–1933) and René Lalique (1860–1945). Influenced by the British avant-garde, Tiffany invented the famous favrile glass, an iridescent glass with incomparable colours. Lalique ●(p. 127), a remarkable glassmaker but also a jeweller and interior designer, was then one of the most eminent exponents of Art Nouveau in France. His glass is a particularly interesting

'The Artistic Crafts' goblet
Lucien Falize, silversmith
Luc-Olivier Merson, painter, designer of the frieze
Chased gold, basse-taille enamel frieze,
red champlevé enamel body,
translucent and opaque enamel on gold
and cloisonné enamel lid
Paris, 1896

'The Secret' casket
Jules Brateau, silversmith
Paul Grandhomme, enameller
Ivory, gold, painted enamel on copper,
mahogany interior
Paris, c.1897

p. 124-25
The 'Wood Drawing Room'
Georges Hoentschel, designer
Adrien Karbowksy, assistant designer
Algerian plane wood, glass,
brass, silk wall fabric
Paris, 1900

123

transition between the naturalism of Art Nouveau and the stylisation of Art Deco. The first of the three large display cases is devoted to porcelain made at Sèvres in 1900. While still producing replicas of the pieces for which it was renowned in the 18th century, the manufactory was quick to adopt Art Nouveau floral decoration with a definite tendency towards stylisation, and forms and reliefs taken directly from the plant realm. The second display highlights the production of the G.D.A. (Gérard, Dufraineux, Abbot) manufactory in Limoges, with a group of porcelain commissioned by Siegfried Bing ●, and pieces from the Copenhagen manufactory, all of whose decoration is high-fired. The third display, echoing Brateau's casket, evokes the role of sculptors in the renaissance of decorative art, with works by Pierre Roche, Alexandre Charpentier and Raoul Larche.

The latter modelled the stunning bronze lamp inspired by the American dancer Loïe Fuller. One of Art Nouveau's great icons, she triumphed at the Universal Exhibition in 1900 in the pavilion specially designed for her by the architect Henri Sauvage, swirling her enormous veils around her in a performance made even more enchanting by electric lighting. She modelled for several sculptors.

The fascination for Japan

Art Nouveau did not emerge fully armed like Athena, out of the thigh of some Zeus of the 'applied arts'. In the late 1860s, a half-naturalist half-poetic tendency influenced by Japanese art gained ascendancy. Flora and fauna—birds, crustaceans, irises, blooming cherry branches, chrysanthemums—were now regarded in a new light. Japanese art had become increasingly well known. The era of the *chinoiserie* had been and gone: it was no longer considered good enough to merely copy picturesque oriental motifs. Three major themes depicted by Hokusai and his contemporaries were taken up by French artists such as Albert Dammouse and Eugène Rousseau: Mount Fuji, the breaking wave and the carp.

In reaction to the invasion of 'all-over decoration', artists gravitated increasingly towards openwork structures playing with space. An undecorated surface was no longer considered a crime. Innovators in this were Félix Bracquemond, Eugène Rousseau and the architect Emile Reiber for Christofle. A set of display cases shows the blooming of this tendency in the 1880s and 1890s ❸.

The dining-room chair by Grasset is confronted by three other chairs by Eugène Gaillard and Hector Guimard ●. Grasset's innovative design is close to the medieval-inspired furniture revisited by Viollet-le-Duc, whereas the others play on the flexuosities of the liana. A major display of ceramics, glass, and precious metalwork illustrates the same radical break with conventional forms.

The rusticity of stoneware

Ernest Chaplet ● (1835–1909), after training at the Sèvres manufactory, abandoned his early, eclectic style to produce vividly coloured stoneware* inspired by his discovery of Norman rustic faience and Japanese stoneware. He worked for Charles Haviland at Auteuil, where he perfected a new barbotine* process. The only decorative features on his most innovative pieces are the streaks in the enamel and the texture of the clay. Paul Gauguin ●(p. 128), whose painting tended to give art back

'Mei Ping' vase
Ernest Chaplet
Porcelain, flamed 'bull's blood' enamel glaze
Choisy-le-Roi, 1899

'Lady in the Snow' vase
Georges de Feure, designer
G.D.A. manufactory
Hard-paste porcelain, high-fired decoration
Paris, Limoges, c.1901

'Two Mermaids' bowl
René Lalique
Moulded, wheel-engraved
and patinated glass; acid-treated interior
France, 1909

Chair
Hector Guimard
Sculpted pearwood, fabric
Paris, 1904

its lost innocence, fired his own ceramics, which he called 'the little products of my high madness'.

Chaplet's Paris workshop was taken over by Auguste Delaherche 👁 (1857–1940), one of the most original ceramicists around the turn of the century, who won a grand prix at the Universal Exhibition in 1900. Most of the pieces on display were donated by the artist and collectors such as Jules Maciet, or bought during his lifetime by the Musée des Arts Décoratifs. He sometimes decorated the superb glazes of his stoneware with stylised motifs such as peacock's feathers. In the stoneware and porcelain workshop he founded at Armentières in 1894, he pursued his experimentation with textures and colours.

The unsurpassable Gallé

Some fifty glass and faience pieces by Emile Gallé provide an overview of the work of the founder the Nancy School and one of the masters of Art Nouveau. Some of the pieces he produced in the 1880s are still derived, more in their decoration than in their form, from 17th and 18th-century ceramics and precious metalwork.

He soon freed himself from these influences, however, and invented new forms which he decorated with camellias, ammonites, snails, dragonflies, seahorses 👁 and irises. Gallé was a learned man, a distinguished botanist and as much a poet as an industrialist, and like the greatest artists of the time, did not regard nature merely as a dictionary of forms. He breathed new vitality into the animals and flowers he captured in molten glass. In 1900, he declared: 'The naturalist document does not move us because the human soul is absent'. His acute perception of natural

Vase
Paul Gauguin, painter and sculptor
Ernest Chaplet, ceramicist
Stoneware, relief decoration,
chased and painted with gold highlighting
Paris, 1886–87

'Flower' dish
Auguste Delaherche
Porcelain
Armentières, 1914

'Peacock Feather' vase
Auguste Delaherche
Glazed stoneware
Paris, c.1889

'Africana' vase
Emile Gallé
Ernest Cardeilhac, silversmith,
after Lucien Bonvallet
Blown glass, glass marquetry, engraved; silver mount
Nancy, 1900

Gallé, magician in glass

Emile Gallé (1846–1904) trained first in Lorraine with his family's ceramics and glass company. Alongside his activities as a faience and furniture designer, he carried out numerous experiments exploring glass's artistic possibilities at the Meisenthal glass factory then at the manufactory he created at Nancy in 1894.

First he enlarged the range of colours of painted enamel and tinted glass, obtaining the most ephemeral nuances. In 1884, he began colouring by adding powders, flakes and other 'dirt' during blowing. Using multiple layers of glass he superimposed different colours in a piece, which he could then acid or wheel-engrave. He added gold leaf and platinum between layers and masterfully exploited effects such a bubbles and iridescence. In 1898, he patented his 'glass marquetry' technique: the insertion of fragments of variable thickness and form while the glass was hot.

These innumerable innovations were all intended to give glass 'the aimable and tragic faces' the artist dreamt of.

'Seahorses' vase
Emile Gallé
Several layers of blown glass, hot-worked,
patina, wheel-engraved
Nancy, 1901

'Carp' vase
Emile Gallé
Blow-moulded and enamelled glass
Paris, 1878

beauty was indistinguishable from the emotion with which he transcribed it.

Also an accomplished chemist, he experimented tirelessly: inclusions between layers of molten glass, coloured elements, gold and platinum leaf, etc. His *Africana* vase ● (p. 129), shown at the Exhibition in 1900, was made using a glass marquetry technique he invented himself: fragments of coloured glass of varying thickness are inserted into the molten glass. Robert de La Sizeranne's words when he left the Universal Exhibition in 1900 could have been specially intended for Gallé: 'The different organs of decorative life blend in this obscure crucible, like the animal, vegetable and mineral realms mingle on the threshold of life.'

In the same room, a display case is devoted to the ceramics of Jean Carriès ● and Albert Dammouse, the iron and silver vases of Lucien Gaillard, and Eugène Rousseau's glass ●. In a more fantastic style, Germain Bapst and Lucien Falize's silver-gilt*, agate and ivory* tea service ● is also influenced by Japan and its colocynths with sinuous stalks.

Eulogy for the stalk

Hector Guimard (1867–1942) built a mansion for the rich industrialist Léon Nozal in rue du Ranelagh in Paris in 1904–1906. The bedroom furniture comes from this house, one of the architect's most harmonious creations ❹. The bed, wardrobe and display cases have an architectural monumentality and their undecorated surfaces emphasise the grain of the pearwood. The finesse of the bases of the chairs and the three-legged pedestal table ● recall Guimard's declaration that 'It is not the flower that I like to take as a decorative element but the stalk'. His extremely purified plant forms full of flowing vitality seem to grow before our very eyes.

In the homes he designed, such as the legendary Castel Henriette, demolished in 1969, Guimard took painstaking care over every detail, even the doorknobs. He proudly described himself as an 'architect of art' and was profoundly convinced that architecture included 'all the other arts without exception'. Pursuing his quest for a total art, he popularised his creations by publishing postcards of the 'Guimard Style'.

The dining room ● Emile Gallé's workshops made around 1904–05 for the Brussels mansion of Edouard Hannon, an engineer who worked at the Solvay factory near Nancy, is one if the great glassmaker's most successful incursions into the furniture realm. Like much of his furniture, the table and sideboards are a combination of sculpture in solid wood and marquetry. The harvest and corn ears illustrate the theme of bread on the serving sideboard, while the sideboard for displaying glassware is decorated with grape-laden vines.

But Emile Gallé did not produce only luxurious pieces. He industrially produced everyday furniture with simplified forms, turning 'low-cost beauty', for a long time considered Utopian, into a reality. His furniture workshops remained in activity until 1914.

Rarely has a style been more criticised than Art Nouveau. Thanks to Guimard's famous Métro station entrances, it had now invaded the public domain. In a story entitled *6 October*, whose action takes place in 1908, Jules Romains describes an apartment in avenue Mozart, furnished 'in the modern style' by Madame de Champcenais, 'who had made the trip to Nancy'. One day, contemplating the mirrored wardrobe, she noticed a disturbing

'Japanese Cascade' vase
Eugène Rousseau
Blown glass, lined and hot-worked, wheel-engraved
Paris, 1884

Twelve-light ceiling lamp
Emile Gallé
Blown glass, lined, acid-engraved; wrought-iron mount
Nancy, c.1904

Pedestal table
Hector Guimard
Moulded and sculpted pearwood
Paris, c.1903

Vase
Jean Joseph Marie Carriès
Stoneware with enamel and gold streaking
Saint-Amand-en-Puisaye, c.1892

Tea service
Germain Bapst
Lucien Falize
Partially gilt silver, ivory, agate
Paris, c.1889

resemblance: 'If I mentally get rid of the mirror itself, then the two uprights and the front of the wardrobe could be mistaken for a Métro station entrance.' Fortunately she had furnished the salon in the Directoire style.

An exceptional wardrobe designed by the Symbolist artist Armand Point (1861–1932), a table with a base sculpted with daisy flowers and foliage ◉ by the painter and architect Edmond-Henri Bellery-Desfontaines (1867–1910), and a musical score cabinet by Henri Becker are all highly personal creations on the margins of Art Nouveau. A picture by Henri Martin (1860–1943), *The Muse*, accentuates the poetic atmosphere of this group, as does the large stained-glass window by Eugène Grasset, *Spring* ◉ (c.1894), whose Symbolist gentleness recalls the diaphanous women painted by Aman-Jean.

Bats and colocynths

A large display case shows the omnipresence of natural themes in decoration but also in the form of the object itself. The mixture of different materials—stoneware, glass, silver, copper—illustrates how the crucible of Art Nouveau succeeded in adapting these forms to all mediums. The first group shows how modern decoration could be used on stylised, even traditional forms. The silver-inlaid copper bowl by the copperware manufacturer Henri Husson ◉ (c.1909) is decorated with a bat with spread wings. Although recalling the structure of ancient Roman goblets, it is decorated with a creature held in contempt in Antiquity and only recently 'rehabilitated' by decadent literature—Robert de Montesquiou's first book of poems *The Bats*, was published in 1891.

The repoussé and gilt* silver chocolate pot Lucien Bonvallet designed for the Cardeilhac company, shown at the Universal Exhibition in 1900, plays on the contrast between floral motifs and polished metal. The turned wood whisk crowned with a bud is inlaid with ivory. It is a rare and exceptionally virtuoso example of Art Nouveau's reinvention of an object emblematic of the gourmet delights and elegance of the 18th century. Lucien Gaillard's slender-necked red-brown and black-patinated bronze *Cabbage* vase offsets the opulence of its natural motifs with its stylised form.

The delicateness of the three gold-rimmed, openwork cloisonné bowls decorated with flowers by Fernand Thesmar is reminiscent of the most exquisite pieces produced by his Japanese counterparts. Rimmed with gold, they are made from translucent enamel using the openwork cloisonné technique: the enamel is not applied to a base and therefore becomes the actual substance of the object. Thin gold lines heighten the motifs and separate the colours.

In the second group, the natural world has taken over the object's form itself. Gourds, colocynths, floral corollas and water-lily leaves with delicately raised edges inspired the forms of the creations of Daum, Dammouse and Lalique. Vases by Maurice Dufrène ◉ (p. 134) and Edmond Lachenal, ewers by Alexandre Bigot ◉ (p. 134) and Majorelle and a gourd by Taxile Doat explore the forms of the vegetable garden in the same way.

A less well-known tendency at the time is illustrated by Henry Cros' moulded glass-paste *Pastorale* vase ◉ (p. 134), coloured in his unmistakable pastel harmonies and mixing naturalist inspiration and echoes of antique bas-reliefs. The Daum vases illustrate several of glass's infinite possibilities:

'Spring'
Eugène Grasset, artist
Félix Gaudin, master glazier
Stained glass, lead
Paris, c.1894

Table
Edmond-Henri Bellery-Desfontaines, designer
Bellanger, cabinetmaker
Sculpted walnut
Paris, 1900

'Bat' bowl
Henri Husson, copperware manufacturer and silversmith
A.A. Hébrard company, founder and silversmith
Repoussé and hammered copper, gold and silver applications
Paris, c.1909

blowing, moulding, hot-working, the insertion of oxides between layers of glass and wheel-ground decoration. The Daum factory began by producing 18th-century-style table services then, from 1891, on Antonin Daum's initiative, it became a genuine laboratory for new forms and technological innovation.

Vase and mount
Maurice Dufrène, designer
Pierre Adrien Dalpayrat, ceramicist
Mount by Lucien Bonvallet,
chased by Ernest Cardeilhac
Flamed stoneware, repoussé
and chased silver mount
Paris, Bourg-la-Reine, 1899–1900

Music and dance

The dancer Loïe Fuller, the ephemeral priestess of modern ballet, already depicted by Raoul Larche, is immortalised here in bronze by Pierre Roche 🉖. The musical curves of the quartet stand and music stands designed by Alexandre Charpentier (1856–1909) and sculpted in honey-coloured hornbeam illustrate the variety of inspiration within Art Nouveau. The sharp, abstract forms of the extraordinary pitcher by Keller Frères 👁 (p. 137) contrast completely with the undulating motifs then triumphing in France.

Ewer
Alexandre Bigot, ceramicist
Edouard Colonna, mount design
Galerie L'Art Nouveau, silversmith
Glazed stoneware, silver-gilt
Paris, 1898

The brilliance of Nancy

The Nancy School, founded by Gallé, gave the capital of Lorraine a prestige comparable to that which it had enjoyed with the court of Stanislas Leczinski, Louis XV's father-in-law. Part of Lorraine, like Alsace, was now German territory so the enclave at Nancy was all the more determined to forge a new, eminently French style. National pride, wounded by the defeat by Prussia in 1870, found a particularly fertile terrain for expression there. At that time, Munich, Vienna, London and Amsterdam were exploring extremely divergent paths in this new decorative universe. As early as 1903, the Union Centrale des Arts

'Pastorale' vase
Henry Cros
Moulded polychrome glass paste
France, c.1895–1900

'The Season of Flowers'
Border of a scenic wallpaper
Prosper Pétrel
Produced by Anciens Ets Desfossé & Karth
Woodblock-printed
France, 1898

Mother Nature

For Art Nouveau artists the study of natural forms was above all a quest for a new vitality. Objects, furniture and buildings were treated as living, growing organisms, not merely as structures to be superficially decorated. The work of the greatest artists, designers and architects—Gallé, Majorelle, Guimard—was infused with the very flux of life. Some, like Gallé, were even accomplished botanists and used modern scientific methods such as the microscope and microphotography in their search for forms. Direct observation of animal and plant forms was complemented by increasingly numerous publications such as Ernst Haeckel's The Artistic Forms of Nature.

These publications provided artists with an extraordinary repertoire of beauty: invertebrates, crustaceans, jellyfish, the reproductive organs of plants, etc. The spiny forms of the monumental gate of the Universal Exhibition in 1900 were inspired by a radiolarian, a microscopic deepsea creature.

Design for a frieze
Hector Guimard
Gouache and watercolour
on brown Canson paper
1902

Sugar spoon
Edouard Colonna, designer
Galerie L'Art Nouveau, silversmith
Silver-gilt
Paris, c.1900

Décoratifs organised an exhibition of the Nancy School in rue de Rivoli.

Apart from Emile Gallé and Victor Prouvé, it was Louis Majorelle, Jacques Gruber and Eugène Vallin who established the prestigious reputation of the Nancy furniture makers **46**. A bedroom suite, a marquetried piano ◉ designed by Victor Prouvé (1903) and an airy, partially gilt* wrought-iron staircase ◉ show the range of this great creator's talent. Taking over his father's furniture-making business in 1879, Majorelle first worked in a frenzied rococo style, a decisive experience which led him naturally towards the fluid, generous forms of Art Nouveau. After working as an engineer at the Daum crystal factory, Jacques Gruber designed furniture for Majorelle and ceramics for the factory at Mougins. His teaching at the school of fine arts in Nancy contributed to the blooming of the new style.

Steinlen's large oil portrait of Madame Dagny Björnson Sautrea (1902) immortalises one of the most famous society hostesses of the period. A friend and patron of Art Nouveau artists such as René Lalique, she was the epitome of the turn-of-the-century woman: no longer the shapely *bourgeoise* straight-jacketed in a corset but a feline creature as supple as a liana. The grey monochrome is a direct homage to the famous *Harmonies* by the Anglo-American painter James Whistler, a major figure in the aesthetic movements in the 1890s.

Purified forms

In the 1910s, Art Nouveau, already a victim of its success, began to be produced industrially—the vulgar forms of these mass-produced pieces became known as the 'noodle style'. So designers tended to purify their forms **47**. Eugène Gaillard's set of Madagascan rosewood nesting tea tables ◉ (1913) is one of the most accomplished examples of this 'return to order'. It illustrates a new quest for elegant simplicity, in which organic forms are subjected to extreme purification. A giltwood* chaise longue by Paul Follot ◉, which he ingeniously gave only one armrest, and a mahogany and ebony wingchair designed by Paul Iribe for the couturier Jacques Doucet, show how this experimentation sometimes erred towards the stylised Neoclassicism of the late 18th century. On the other hand, Louis Sorel's tea table (c.1910), whose top fans out, foreshadows the formal audacity of the Cubists in the 1920s. These first experiments led straight into Art Deco.

Nesting tea tables
Eugène Gaillard
Padouk wood base, rosewood veneer
Paris, c.1913

'Honesty' staircase
Louis Majorelle
Wrought iron, polished steel, gilt bronze,
brass, wood, imitation stone paint
Nancy, model created 1903

Chaise longue
Paul Frédéric Follot
Sculpted and gilt beech,
silk fabric with peacock feather motif
Paris, c.1912

Ewer
Keller Frères
Silver–gilt
Paris, c.1900

Baby grand piano
Victor Prouvé, designer
Louis Majorelle, decoration
Sculpted mahogany base, wood marquetry
Nancy, 1903

Art Deco

In 1918, at the end of the First World War, France was decimated: 1,400,000 dead, 750,000 invalids. The United States and Great Britain proved loath to ensure the strict application of the Treaty of Versailles weakening Germany.

Due to the reconstruction effort and the industrial expansion that had begun at the beginning of the century, the 1920s was a period of unprecedented economic growth. Consumerism progressed, stimulated by advertising and credit. The West, and particularly the United States, the world's largest economy, began to believe in never-ending prosperity. The Colonial Exhibition in 1931 marked the peak of the 'French Empire'. The Wall Street Crash on 24 October 1929 pitched capitalism into turmoil. International commerce collapsed. In Germany, the banking system was annihilated. Totalitarian states embarked on policies of territorial expansion.

The first regular French radio programmes began in 1920. Hitler was the first to use radio as a political propaganda tool. There were considerable technological advances in aviation: in 1920, the first plane flew above 10,000 metres altitude and the first night flight took place in 1922.

Walter Gropius founded the Bauhaus in Weimar in 1919, abolishing the distinctions between architecture, the decorative arts and the fine arts. Mies van der Rohe designed the first European skyscrapers in 1919. In his *Plan Voisin de Paris* (1925), Le Corbusier developed his concept of a modern metropolis composed of lines of high, cruciform tower blocks. As the world was assimilating Freud's explorations of the subconscious, in 1924 André Breton published *Manifeste du Surréalisme*. The Surrealist movement, a galaxy of writers and poets, asserted man's poetic nature and the power of the subconscious.

⑨
⑧
⑦
⑥
⑤
④
③
②
①

1919
Creation of the League of Nations at the instigation of President Wilson.

1927
The first 'talkie' film:
The Jazz Singer.

1928
Alexander Fleming discovers penicillin.

Chest of drawers
Paul Iribe
(detail, see p. 141)

Art Deco

The war was over. Paris was reinventing luxury and discovering jazz. Fashionable women were now slender-limbed, wore their hair short, and smoked. Automobiles went faster, planes flew further. In the home the radio meted out 'the news'. Mallet-Stevens and Cavalcanti designed the sets of Marcel L'Herbier's film *L'Inhumaine* (1924). Art Nouveau was dead, vive l'Art Deco!

Cubism for all

Elsewhere, the great return to geometry had begun long ago. In Scotland in the 1890s, the Glasgow Four, led by Charles Rennie Mackintosh, had invented the stylised rose that would become one of the emblems of the Art Deco style. They designed solid, functional, soberly but luxuriously decorated furniture. Their influence was felt as far as Vienna, where the Secession was at the peak of its glory. When the City of Paris commissioned Guimard to design its Métro station entrances, Vienna asked Otto Wagner to build its own underground railway system.

But by 1913, as Paris was discovering the tango and Cubism was already in full swing, all the elements of a new, rigorous, modern style were in place: the return of the straight line, abstract, stylised decoration, bright and violently contrasting colours.

But before 1914, a few isolated initiatives had shown the way **47**: chairs designed by Paul Follot **👁**, Adrien Karbowsky, Louis Süe and Clément Mère imposed the return to simple, solid forms inspired by the Neoclassical furniture of the 1780s–1800s. Instead of the indigenous woods favoured by Art Nouveau, Art Deco cabinetmakers preferred exotic wood veneers **👁**. Giltwood* was also very popular. Commissions and state purchases for ministries and embassies were also a rich source of income until the 1930s.

In the 1910s Emile Decœur and Emile Lenoble covered their ceramics with stylised flowers, and François-Emile Décorchemont moulded pure forms minimally decorated with relief ornaments.

Curiously, one of the precursors of Art Deco was not an architect or even a cabinet-maker but the couturier Paul Poiret. Not content with merely revolutionising fashion—he had done away with the corset and invented the modern female figure—he turned his hand to interior decoration.

In 1910, Poiret met the Viennese architect Josef Hoffmann, cofounder of the Wiener Werkstätte (Vienna Workshop), whose aim was to change every aspect of the environment from the teaspoon to furniture, fabrics and the postcard. Hoffmann may well have instilled in Poiret the ambition to do the same in France. In 1911 he asked Raoul Dufy to design fabrics for him, and the same year founded his own interior design company, Martine. In 1912, a group of artists, including Raymond Duchamp-Villon and André Mare showed their Cubist House, an attempt to adapt a toned-down Cubism to the living space, at the Salon d'Automne.

A hymn to beauty

The Prince Louis de Polignac Donation has enabled the museum to show three rooms from one of the most refined interiors designed in the 1920s, the apartment of the couturière Jeanne Lanvin in rue Barbet-de-Jouy in Paris, decorated in 1924–25 and dismantled in 1965 **48**. With her infallible instinct, 'Madame Lanvin' chose Armand Albert Rateau (1882–1938), a highly individual designer and disciple

Chest of drawers
Paul Iribe
Mahogany, tulipwood, slate,
green-tinted shagreen, ebony
Paris, c.1912

Chair
Paul Frédéric Follot
French maple, amaranth
and ebony marquetry, leather
Paris, c.1912

'Fauns' screen
André Mare, painter
Compagnie des arts français
Gloss paint on parchment
mounted on wood,
gilt brass frame
Paris, c.1920

of Georges Hoentschel, to decorate this place of supreme elegance: rich but unostentatious, modern but not discordant, bourgeois but not petty. The bathroom, with its niche decorated with a bas-relief in staff, bath carved out of a block of Hauteville marble, and alabaster and patinated bronze lamps, is definitely the most entrancing of the three rooms. The bronze furniture ◉, with its disconcertingly fanciful mixture of pine cones, birds, fishes and daisies, is particularly original. Yet there is also a certain gravity: the candelabras could have lit some temple for the worship of beauty. Rateau succeeded in reconciling the inspiration of the great civilisations of Antiquity in his original, floral creations symbolising a timeless 'sweetness of living'.

In the bedroom ◉ (p. 144–45), the blue silk-upholstered chairs have the curves of the Second Empire style, while in the boudoir the exquisite brown lacquer* and gilt* bronze chest of drawers could almost have come from Marie-Antoinette's apartment. Rateau became director of Lanvin-Décoration in 1921 and designed the Lanvin boutiques. He also designed the decoration of the Daunou theater and the Pavillon de l'Elégance at the 1925 Exhibition.

A French style

Another complete ensemble, the dining room ◉ designed by Louis Süe and André Mare, founders of the Compagnie des Arts Français in 1919, is just as steeped in tradition ㊾. Made in rosewood and blackened wood for Monsieur and Madame Pierre Girod in 1921, its forms are reminiscent of the massive and comfortable furniture of the reign of Louis-Philippe. Many other designers made similar forays into the past in their search for a new, specifically French style.

In the second half of the 19th century, the dining room was furnished with darker woods and fabrics, considered a more suitable backdrop for the sparkle of crystal* and the whiteness of porcelain* and faience*, and therefore also the food and drink. The room is filled with a longing for the bourgeois life of yesteryear. During the war, Süe and Mare worked in an aviation factory and had their collection of cheap modern furniture, sold by catalogue, made by the same factory.

A magician with glass

Maurice Marinot ◉ began as a painter, exhibiting with the Fauves at the Salon des Indépendants and the Salon d'Automne until 1911. He then devoted himself entirely to glass, of which he became one of the incontestable masters. He soon abandoned his repertoire of enamelled figurative elements for solid, simple forms, allowing the glass itself to 'sing'. His blown glass vases, enamelled, sprinkled with gold flakes and wheel or acid-engraved, immediately became highly sought-after collector's pieces. Some look like they were carved out of ice, others suggest the mysterious effervescence of a liquid. Most of the pieces on display here were bequeathed by the politician Louis Barthou. An extremely learned man and a passionate art collector, he was assassinated with King Alexander I of Yugoslavia in Marseille in 1934.

Pear-shaped bottle
Maurice Marinot
Blown glass, inset decoration,
hot-worked, wheel-engraved
France, 1930

Chaise longue
Armand Albert Rateau, designer
Baguès Frères, bronze founder
Cast, antique green-patinated bronze
Paris, c.1925

Dining room
Compagnie des Arts Français
Louis Süe, architect
André Mare, painter
Paris, 1921

p. 144–45
Jeanne Lanvin's bedroom
Armand Albert Rateau
Armless chair: moulded
and painted beech, silk
Alcove bed: sculpted
and painted wood, gilt
bronze, silk
Wall lamp: green antique-
patinated bronze, silk,
glass, pearls
Paris, 1925

Art Deco

The glory of Paris in 1925

The idea for an International Exhibition of the Decorative Arts in Paris had taken shape in 1906. Initially planned for 1915, postponed until 1916 then abandoned because of the war, it finally took place in 1925 **⑤⓪**.

Paris was obsessed with recovering its former aesthetic hegemony: Germany had been defeated militarily but it now had to be in the luxury arts. The 'triumph of French taste' was hailed by the voluntarily nationalist press. Raymond Escholier wrote: '[...] after a long eclipse, the native virtues of our race—order, measure, clarity, discipline—have decisively won the day. Gone the anarchy of 1900 and the hegemony of Munich. While our painters have only one concern, [...] a return to the art of Poussin, our interior designers and cabinetmakers, whilst keeping the feeling of modern life, do not hesitate to embrace the tradition of Louis XVI and the Directoire.'

Urged by Paul Léon, director of the Ecole des Beaux-Arts, the Société des Artistes Décorateurs decided to participate, choosing 'A French Embassy' as its theme. Breaking with the traditional, pompous style of official reception rooms (except for Dunand's sumptuous black and silver smoking room), the ambassador's private apartment was in a more innovative style.

Clock
Louis Cartier, jeweller
Maurice Coüet, clockmaker
Sculpted white jade, onyx, diamonds, coral, mother-of-pearl, gold
Paris, 1927

Indecent curves

The *Chambre de Madame* in the French Embassy pavilion contained one of the most extraordinary pieces of furniture of the Roaring Twenties, André Groult's *Anthropomorphic Chiffonnier* **◉**. Curved, as the designer himself admitted, 'to the point of indecency', it is covered entirely

'Anthropomorphic Chiffonnier'
André Groult
Mahogany covered with shagreen, ivory, silver-plated hinges
Paris, c.1925

Architecture at the 1925 Exhibition

The visitor who went through one of the four monumental gates of the International Exhibition of the Decorative Arts entered what at first sight seemed like a fantastic architectural display. The aim above all was to be 'modern' and this credo had given the ensemble a certain unity. All the pavilions had the Cubist volumes and geometry then in fashion. But many, like the pavilions of the department stores or the Compagnie des Arts Français, had profusely decorated these rigid structures. Ruhlmann's 'Hôtel du Collectionneur', designed by Patout, was imposingly pure in its classicism. Apart from the designs by Mallet-Stevens, the modernist movement was brilliantly represented by the Lyon pavilion, built by Tony Garnier, and Le Corbusier, Jeanneret and Ozenfant's Esprit Nouveau pavilion, built entirely with standardised components and whose 'poverty' shocked the critics. The avant-garde De Stijl group had been excluded by the Dutch commission, which opted for a more traditional pavilion, which Van Doesburg described as a 'black farm, absurd, sombre like a church'.

Project for the Tourism pavilion
Robert Mallet-Stevens
Gouache on paper
Paris, 1925

'Hôtel du Collectionneur'
Pierre Patout, architect
Jacques-Emile Ruhlmann, interior designer
Paris, 1925

The 'Esprit Nouveau' pavilion
Le Corbusier
Paris, 1925

with shagreen*, a material that had become extremely popular again, and has ivory fittings. The room was decorated in a range of greys, pinks and blues echoing the pictures by Marie Laurencin. These warm, muted colour harmonies perfectly offset Groult's flesh-coloured furniture.

A clock ◉ (p. 146) by Louis Cartier and Maurice Coüet epitomises the insolent luxury that characterises so many of the creations of this period of newfound peace and prosperity. Made in sculpted white jade, onyx, coral, mother-of-pearl and gold and inset with diamonds, it seems to embody some fabulous dream of the Far East, or some caprice of a Chinese emperor seen through a haze of opium smoke.

Crowned with its daring, luminous cupola, Pierre Chareau's office-library ◉ (p. 150–51) has been reconstructed here in the museum with its original furniture and carpet designed by Jean Lurçat ⑤. An architect and the designer of Doctor Dalsace's famous Glass house in rue Saint-Guillaume in Paris (1931), Chareau's furniture has strict, powerfully lines, emphasised by dark rosewood veneer. The desk's bevelled top, as one can imagine, is not very practical—papers would have a tendency to slip off it. The columns supporting the cupola are covered with palmwood, as are the fan-like slat blinds which keep out the sun during the day, when electric light was not necessary. Hanging not far from the office-library is *Woman in Red* ◉ (1927) by Jean Dupas, one of the fashionable artists in the 1920s.

Impeccable forms

Further on, a panorama of the various movements in the decorative arts in 1925. One can easily recognise the full forms of Jean Puiforcat's silverware, including the famous vegetable dish ◉ with a jade ring handle, donated by him in 1926. Other examples of the metalworking crafts are the pieces by Jean Després, one of the most extraordinary silversmiths of the period, and the Dane Christian Fjerdingstad, who created a line of rigorously formal objects for Christofle.

In ceramics*, Suzanne Lalique's creations reinterpret the French porcelain of yesteryear with great freshness, while Emile Lenoble's coarse-textured stoneware could almost have been made by some civilisation several thousand years ago. The great names of Lalique and Daum ◉ are present among the glassware. During this period Antonin Daum was fond of playing on the transparency of crystal, heightening it with gold and insetting it with powders or adding coloured glass applications.

The remarkable glass paste vase by François Décorchemont ◉, made using the lost wax casting process, belonged to Louis Barthou. Décorchemont also made the set of bowls and dishes using the same process, which imbues the translucent glass with all the massive plasticity of stoneware.

'Lady in Red'
Jean Dupas
Oil on parqueted wood
Paris, 1927

Vegetable dish
Jean Emile Puiforcat
Repoussé and chased silver, jade ring
Paris, c.1925

Vase
Daum manufactory
Blown, bubbled and hot-worked glass
Nancy, 1924

'Vase with two leaf handles'
François Décorchemont
Lost wax-cast glass paste
France, 1925

p. 150–51
Office-library for 'A French Embassy'
Pierre Chareau
Desk: rosewood veneer, mahogany, oak, steel
Panelling: beech, palmwood veneer
Paris, 1925

Jacques Doucet,
couturier and patron of the arts

By purchasing or commissioning works from some of the greatest creators of his time, the French couturier Jacques Doucet became one of the most influential figures in the art world in the 1920s. Advised by Louis Aragon and André Breton, the man who would amass the extraordinary book collection now named after him, had prudently and superbly furnished his mansion in rue Spontini in Paris with 18th-century furniture, objets d'art and pictures.

In 1912, however, he auctioned his entire 18th-century collection to devote himself entirely to the art of his time. His widow and heirs donated some of the furniture in his apartment in avenue du Bois (now avenue Foch), decorated by Paul Poiret, and subsequently in his mansion and studio apartment in Neuilly ❷: the small shagreen* or parchment desk by Pierre Legrain and Jean-Charles Moreux, the capeskin and parchment piece by Paul-Louis Mergier and Marcel Coard's ebony*-veneered and lacquered display case ◉. Coard later considered this piece, dated 1914–15, whose sides curve outwards to contain a large Macassar ebony-veneered circle, to be his most accomplished work. It is gold-lacquered inside. Pierre Legrain, who worked with Paul Iribe for the satirical paper *Le Témoin*, designed some of the most original pieces in this legendary ensemble, including the palmwood*, lacquered and parchment-covered 'African' chair ◉ evoking a tribal throne. Legrain, who orchestrated much of the work in Doucet's studio apartment, supervised its decoration.

This furniture gives an idea of one of the century's most influential interiors, whose

Display case
Marcel Coard
Metal and oak structure, Macassar ebony and mother-of-pearl veneer, gold-lacquered interior and shelves, ivory feet and shelf supports, glass
Paris, 1914–15

African chair
Pierre Legrain
Sculpted palmwood, lacquered decoration, parchment and sheepskin upholstery
Paris, c.1924

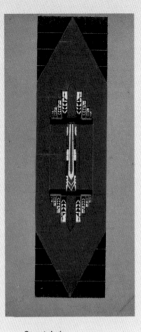

Carpet design
Gustave Miklos
Gouache on greyish-brown paper
Paris, 1921

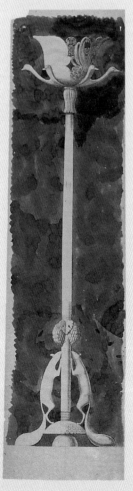

Standard lamp design
Paul Plumet, designer
Armand Albert Rateau, interior designer
Black ink and wash on tracing paper
Paris, c.1920

Haute Couture and Art Deco

Three great names in haute couture left their mark on the Art Deco style. Jacques Doucet, the couturier of the 1900 'ornate woman', simplified the lines of his dresses around 1910 but above all in 1912 moved out of his mansion decorated in the 18th century style to live in an avant-garde décor. 'Believe me,' he said, 'the contemporary woman can only be beautiful in a modern décor.' He enlisted the services of promising young designers such as Legrain, Iribe and Coard, defining his role as 'seducing a few highly gifted young people with the joys of risk.'

Paul Poiret, influenced by the aesthetics of the Ballets Russes, saw woman as a languid sultana. He did away with the corset but gathered in dresses at the bottom. In 1911, he was the first couturier to have his own perfume house, Rosine. The same year, influenced by the Viennese artists of the Wiener Werkstätte, he created Atelier Martine, which produced wallpaper, embroidery, upholstery, porcelain and furniture. Nicknamed the Martines, the young women whom Poiret trained there worked with Dufy on the decoration of the three barges he presented at the 1925 Exhibition.

That year, Jeanne Lanvin was one of the rare creators to have the honour of showing in the Pavillon de l'Elégance. The embodiment of 'French excellence', she presided over the Exhibition's XX class, devoted to fashion. With Armand Albert Rateau, who decorated her Paris mansion, she created Lanvin-Décoration, which decorated the Lanvin boutiques in rue du Faubourg-Saint-Honoré in Paris and the Daunou theatre. Jeanne Lanvin and Rateau shared the same taste for rare materials and showed great freedom in their reinterpretation of the styles of the past.

lapis lazuli skirting boards, marquetry parquet, large lacquer panels and walls hung with pigskin fixed with gold studs were worthy of a sybarite. And of course there were pictures by the great masters: Douanier Rousseau's *The Snake Charmer* and Manet's *On the Beach* (both now in the Musée d'Orsay), and works by Marie Laurencin, Braque and Picasso.

There were also less well-known names, reflecting the complexity of the Parisian artistic landscape in the 1920s and 30s. Apart from the picture by Jean Dupas mentioned above, Roger de La Fresnaye's *The Factory at La-Ferté-sous-Jouarre* illustrates the vitality of French figurative painting between the wars, tinged with the boldness of Cubism.

The Ruhlmann influence

Jacques-Emile Ruhlmann was incontestably the leading cabinetmaker in Paris in the 1920s. Like the artists whose services Doucet enlisted, he combined decorative art and luxury in creations using rare materials. In 1910, at the Salon d'Automne, he showed furniture influenced by late 18th-century French furniture, then after the war founded his own interior design company. He triumphed at the 1925 Exhibition with his *Hôtel du Collectionneur (Collector's Mansion)* ● (p. 147), designed by his friend the architect Pierre Patout and resembling his own residence.

To decorate this grandiose pavilion, Ruhlmann commissioned artists such as Edgar Brandt for the wrought iron, Joseph Bernard for the bas-reliefs on the facade, Jean Dupas for the painting above the fireplace in the large drawing room, and Jean Puiforcat for the silverware. The Macassar ebony* and ivory* lady's roll-top desk, one

of which was in the small drawing room, the ambassador's desk and the cabinet inlaid with ivory ● eloquently demonstrate why this cabinetmaker was immediately compared to greatest 18th-century masters such as Riesener and Weisweiler. The lady's writing table ● is more daring in conception, combining kingwood, capeskin, silver and snakeskin.

Eulogy for the machine

Furthering the great tradition of French cabinetmaking in their technical perfection and use of rare materials, the master pieces commissioned by Doucet and Ruhlmann's great pieces were confronted with the most radical tendency in decorative art at that time, influenced by the rigour of the new architecture.

A podium is devoted to the office furniture of Robert Mallet-Stevens ●, one of the key figures of the French architectural avant-garde. At Paul Poiret's château at Mézy, at the legendary Villa Noailles at Hyères and the famous Villa Cavrois at Croix, recently saved from ruin, Mallet-Stevens drew inspiration from modernist Vienna and the Bauhaus, founded in Weimar in 1919 by the architect Walter Gropius.

He not only 'furnished' the 1925 Exhibition with reinforced cement Cubist trees sculpted by the Martel brothers and an extraordinary Tourism Pavilion whose campanile thumbed its nose at the grandiloquent architecture of the Grand Palais, but apparently also used his influence to ensure the presence of Le Corbusier's famous *Esprit Nouveau* pavilion ● (p. 147), co-designed by Pierre Jeanneret and Amédée Ozenfant. The furniture of its office was entirely made from metal tubing and Duco synthetic lacquer.

Vase
Jean Dunand
Copper, eggshell lacquer
Paris, c.1924

Cabinet
Jacques-Emile Ruhlmann
Amaranth veneer, ivory and ebony marquetry, ivory inlay
Paris, c.1922–23

Lady's writing table
Jacques-Emile Ruhlmann
Kingwood veneer, tobacco brown capeskin,
chromed bronze, ivory, Macassar ebony, snakeskin
Paris, 1933

Desk
Robert Mallet-Stevens
Stamped sheet metal, Duco lacquer,
nickel-plated metal tubing, leather top,
silvered metal compartments
Paris, c.1927

The large lacquered screen by Jean Dunand was in the dining room.

As with reinforced concrete in architecture, the use of metal in furniture enabled designers to abandon traditional structures without compromising solidity. The desktop is joined to the chests of drawers below by a single central strip of steel, leaving space for dossiers and papers underneath, and instead of legs the chests of drawers have a tubular metal base. In Mallet-Stevens' furniture the quest for functionality never takes precedence over elegance. 'The clear and logical forms of the new furniture, in which mechanics intervenes, and knowledge of automobiles and planes, [...] the ease with which one wants to have everything in order with the minimum of effort, and air, which has just been invented thanks to sport [...] plead in favour of a modern habitat, modern in its practicality and aesthetics,' the architect wrote in 1931.

The reign of metal

Pierre Chareau and Ruhlmann himself were both tempted by metal furniture. Thonet Frères, a specialist in bentwood furniture since the mid-19th century, and Atelier Primavera, the design studio of the Grands Magasins du Printemps, were also seduced by the sirens of this nickel and chrome-plated avant-garde. Thonet produced the famous *MR 533* leather and tubular steel chair designed by Mies Van der Rohe in 1927, whose precarious balance is still just as spectacular today. Marcel Breuer, one of the pioneers of tubular furniture with his *Wassily* chair, and who directed the furniture workshop at the Bauhaus from 1925, is represented by an aluminium chaise longue designed in 1933.

In 1929, a group of designers and architects influenced by the theories of the Bauhaus, led by René Herbst and Robert Mallet-Stevens and including Pierre Chareau, Eileen Gray ✪, Charlotte Perriand, Le Corbusier and Jean Burckhalter, founded the Union des Artistes Modernes (UAM).

They held their first Salon in the Marsan pavilion in 1930. Entirely logically, the pieces on the podium here are all metal or nickel or chrome-plated steel ❺. Among the mythical objects in this group are Herbst's 1931 chaise longue ✪, whose spidery form seems frozen in some gymnastic exercise. This type of hygienic, easy to clean furniture was adopted in the late 20s by restaurants, bars and hotels such as *Le Bar sous le toit*, designed by Charlotte Perriand.

Contrasting completely with these pieces destined for a wide public, the minimalist elegance of the Princess Aga Khan's dressing table, designed by Herbst in 1932, shows how these materials can be adapted to the most prestigious commissions. Its true luxury consists in the extreme precision of its assembly, the perfection of its polish and the purity of its entirely undecorated forms.

One of the unique pieces on display in this room is the centrepiece by Puiforcat ✪, a combination of precious materials—rock crystal, silver, and sand-engraved glass—on a table by Dominique. The centrepiece, a traditional feature of luxurious tables, is shaped like a turbine, and recalls Le Corbusier's eulogy of the machine in *L'Art décoratif moderne* in 1925: 'The machine is all geometry. Geometry is our great creation and delights us. The machine shines its polished steel disks, spheres and cylinders before our eyes [...] with a theoretical precision and acuity that nature could never show us.' The jeweller

Cigarette case
Raymond Templier
Silver, aluminium, lacquer
Paris, c.1923

'Coiffeuse'
Eileen Gray
Oregon pine, plywood, cork, aluminium, glass,
traces of turquoise blue paint
Paris, 1926–29

Centrepiece
Jean Emile Puiforcat
Silver, rock crystal
Paris, 1930

Chaise longue
René Herbst
Chrome-plated steel tubing, parkerised steel springs
Paris, c.1931

Raymond Templier, a member of the UAM, also showed the same mechanist inspiration in his series of priceless lacquered silver and aluminium cigarette cases ◉ (p. 157).

The antithesis of this angular modernity is the generously curved silver, ivory and rosewood* breakfast service designed by Jean Tétard and made by Tétard Frères. It was shown at the Colonial Exhibition in Paris in 1931, and with its very materials flaunted the riches of the French colonial empire. A set of Baccarat crystal and chrome-plated metal glasses, another designed by Jean Luce for the Saint-Louis crystal factory, and Luce's faience *Rectangular Service* ◉ convey the same aspiration in the 1930s towards a simpler, fuller and more massive interpretation of Art Deco forms.

'Rectangular Service'
Jean Luce, designer
HBCM manufactory
Faience
Paris, Montereau, 1932

Cabinet
Clément Mère
Macassar ebony, embossed and lacquered leather,
tinted ivory, pearl, opal and box inlay
Paris, c.1913

An exotic luxury

The austere forms and rational construction of Art Deco furniture, and the importance given to the interplay of volumes and flat surfaces, seem to have pushed certain great designers towards increasingly rich materials. Just as Empire furniture had given pride of place to beautifully grained mahogany*, Art Deco exploited the sombre striations of rosewood*, kingwood, palmwood and Macassar ebony*, the shimmering ripples of lemonwood and the pebbledash effects of burred* amboine. The deep brilliance of lacquer conjured up the mysteries of the Far East, and parchment's fragile epidermis and the grain of shagreen introduced a hint of barbarism. One of the pioneers in the use of sumptuous materials was the luxury goods manufacturer Clément Mère, who even tinted and gilded ivory* and tattooed it with strange abstract motifs. These priceless substances came from the French colonies, of which the 1931 Colonial Exhibition was the last dazzling showcase.

Chair
Clément Rousseau
Rosewood, green-tinted shagreen,
ivory, silk
Paris, c.1921

Modern

The totalitarian regimes of Mussolini in Italy and Hitler in Germany were becoming increasingly threatening. The Bauhaus was disbanded in 1933 and most of its members emigrated. Gropius went to England then the United States. The 30s were troubled times in France too. Demonstrations became more frequent and were often brutally repressed.

Léon Blum, the leader of the Socialists, became head of the Popular Front in 1936. The Matignon Agreement enabled the French government and the trade unions to embark on an unprecedented series of social reforms. In the summer of 1936, after the introduction of two weeks annual paid holiday, the first phenomena of mass tourism began. In Paris in 1937, the International Exhibition of Arts and Techniques in Modern Life reflected the exacerbation of nationalism in Europe. The exhibition was dominated by the colossal pavilions of the USSR and Nazi Germany. In the Spanish pavilion, Picasso showed *Guernica,* inspired by Franco's bombing of the ill-fated Basque town that year. Although France played her part in the victory alongside the Allies, she emerged from the Second World War a weakened nation, no longer the major power she had been at the beginning of the century.

France was at an economic standstill and her colonial empire weakened, but the Marshall plan accelerated reconstruction and enabled French households to benefit from technological advances improving everyday life. Families drove around in the economical Citroën 2CV and Renault 4CV. In 1945, women were given the vote. The social struggles of yesteryear died away and the consumer society was born.

In a period dominated by ideologies, André Malraux, Cultural Affairs Minister in 1959, wanted to make art 'the substitute of all transcendences'. In the cinema, the New Wave used documentary, the personal diary and reportage in its quest for an existential reality.

1943

Jean-Paul Sartre publishes *Being and Nothingness,* his major philosophical work.

1946

The beginning of the reconstruction of Le Havre by Auguste Perret.

1954

The defeat of the French at Dien Bien Phu marks the end of the Indochina War. Beginning of the Algerian War.

1961

Inauguration of Orly Airport.

'Radiaver'
(detail, see p. 163)

Modern

Maurice Ravel's free and varied score for *The Child and the Enchantments,* performed for the first time in 1925, heralded the changes of the years come. He blended medieval polyphony, *bel canto,* the blues, the foxtrot, the jig and the pavane in a libertarian and devastating exaltation, a lyrical fantasy foreshadowing in music two major characteristics of the decorative arts from the 30s to the 50s.

There was first of all the extraordinary diversity of genres and tendencies. As Ravel had done in his 'orchestral constellation', designers mixed plastic and metal, like architects did concrete, metal and wood. Modernity was above all the certainty that nothing was inert, that everything had to move, and that what is isolated can be combined.

This creative mobility was above all the result of the new mobility of people and works. The first motorways were built in the 1930s. By the 1950s air transport had become banal, and photography was making the world's artistic heritage available to all.

Feeling threatened by the uncertainties of arts which were evolving so quickly, some feared the 'crisis of the mind' Paul Valéry wrote about in 1919, and turned towards national heritage and traditional craftsmanship. Others, however, who in 1929 formed the Union des Artistes Modernes (UAM), wanted to 'create forms and objects adapted to their use'. A vigorous debate between ancients and moderns began, and lasted until the late 1950s.

A functionalist modernity

In the 1930s, the modernist spirit was still embodied in Paris by the artists federated under the banner of the UAM. The functionalism of modern art was an expression of a refusal of decoration and the superfluous. At a time when the effects of unemployment and the drop in purchas-ing power were exacerbating political and social unrest, a militant commitment to a 'social art' seemed crucial. The backward-looking, nostalgic faction yearning for the 'beautiful crafts of France', followed in Ruhlmann's footsteps, attempting to adapt the grand tradition of French cabinetmaking to purified forms.

The International Exhibition of Arts and Techniques in Paris, inaugurated during the Popular Front in 1937, served as a showcase for these contradictory tendencies ❺❹. It glorified the artistic crafts, but also aviation, the magic of electricity and new applications of glass and rubber. The architect René Coulon (1907–97) host of the UAM pavilion, also co-designed the pavilion of the Saint-Gobain glass company with Jacques Adnet. Over a hundred tons of moulded glass were used in its concrete structure.

The pavilion's furniture was also made of toughened glass, like the Securit glass chair ●, whose transparent components harmoniously match the sober leather-upholstered seat. Glass blends just as harmoniously with metal in the extraordinary *Radiaver* radiator-lamp ●, also made by Saint-Gobain. René Herbst (1891–1982), who trained as an architect and, like Coulon, became an interior designer, declared: 'It is the object's use which motivates the material and not the material which adapts itself to the object.' The originality of his pearwood, mahogany and metal *Multipurpose wall cabinet* ●, lined with leather inside, is an illustration of this.

Armchair
René Coulon
Hagnauer, publisher; Saint-Gobain, manufacturer
Thermo-formed and strengthened glass, leather
1938

'Radiaver' radiator–lamp
Saint-Gobain, manufacturer
Strengthened glass, moulded glass base, metal
1937

'Multipurpose wall cabinet'
René Herbst
Metal, pearwood, mahogany, leather
1937

Modern

The sharp forms of André Hermant (1908-78) are represented here by a simple, pure table ◉ with a red gloss painted sheet metal frame and plate glass top. This architect and member of the UAM, for whom he designed the architecture gallery and the bookshop at the 1937 Exhibition, also designed the Rubber pavilion. It was he who first formulated the notion of 'useful forms' in the late 1940s.

Tradition revisited

Presented at the 1937 Exhibition in the Private Architecture pavilion, the *Chambre de Madame* (Madame's bedroom) illustrates the best of the great French tradition that continued into the 1950s.

It was an expression of its designer, the cabinetmaker and sculptor André Arbus (1903–69) desire to 'free myself from a too mechanical and too abstract spirit'. The forms of its ivory-lacquered furniture are flowing and majestic. The dressing table and chest of drawers are covered with ivory-coloured parchment. The softness of the materials, forms and colours creates an intimate atmosphere of respectable luxury—a far cry from the angular coldness of metal and glass. Evolving in the late 1940s towards a simplified version of the forms of the 18th century, Arbus designed furniture for embassies and national palaces such as the apartment for foreign sovereigns at the Château de Rambouillet.

The only buildings built for the 1937 Exhibition still standing are the Palais de Chaillot and the two Museums of Modern Art (now the Palais de Tokyo and the Musée d'Art Moderne de la Ville de Paris). They were an attempt to combine

Candlesticks
Jean Després
Silver-plated metal, hammered and polished
1937

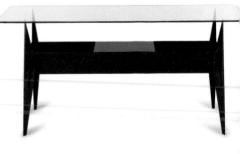

Bookshop table
André Hermant
Painted sheet metal, glass
1937

'Paris 1937'
Leonetto Cappiello
Colour lithograph
1937

'1937 International Exhibition'
Jean Carlu
Colour lithograph
1937

1937: industry and the 'beautiful crafts'

With 44 nations represented, over 300 palaces and pavilions and 31 million visitors, the 1937 Exhibition was the last great event of its kind to be held in Paris. An 'International' rather than 'Universal' exhibition, it aimed above all to affirm France's supremacy in the luxury goods industries. Its theme was the 'arts and techniques', and it included an extremely wide range of works and products. The Aeronautics pavilion, the Light pavilion, the exceptional pavilion of the Saint-Gobain company, designed by René Coulon and Jacques Adnet, the UAM pavilion and the site's spectacular electric illuminations all celebrated industrial modernity. In contrast, the Crafts Centre presented the work of the Sèvres, Gobelins and La Monnaie national manufactories, insisting on the timelessness of 'France's beautiful crafts', far from the dangers of the 'standardisation of the factory'.

André Arbus, an advocate of a new French classicism, prophesied the death of the 'cut-price Cubism' and 'tube chairs' of 1925. This return to the decorativeness and grace of the 18th century, well in evidence in the Artistes Décorateurs and Private Architecture pavilions, was no longer considered a crime.

Design for a music room
André Arbus
Gouache drawing
c.1937

the clear volumes and smooth surfaces of modernism with a purified Neoclassicism, in a style which the architects themselves described as Neo-Roman.

Between rigour and primitivism

A curiosity cabinet contains a selection of metal, glass and ceramic objects. Although new materials and iconoclast assemblages would be out of place here, the designers, in their use of traditional materials, showed a profound desire for renewal. Jean Puiforcat, who exhibited in his own pavilion, was fond of softening the coldness of silver by associating it with unexpected motifs. The exact forms of his soup dish ● are warmed only by sparing use of gilding. He heightened a vase as beautiful as a chalice with a spiral line of silver like a spring.

Jean Després ● (p. 164), also a silversmith and also sensitive to industrial forms, hammered silver like a boilermaker and subjected the precious metal to the rigours of strict geometry. In a large vase ●, Aristide Colotte (1885–1959) combined a massif, rounded blown-glass body and two cut-glass handles whose strict geometry evokes the hardness of metal. In the same way, the *African Vase* by Jean Besnard (1889–1958) combines the primitive and coarse appearance of terracotta and notched motifs evoking the industrial world.

On the threshold of the 1950s, this geometry dissolved in soft, organic forms, as in the blown and hot-worked glass dish ● by André Thuret (1898–1965). The simple outlines of the glass of Jean Sala ● (1895–1976) seem like a softened echo of ancient Rome. But as André Hermant dryly wrote: 'There are no rea-

sons why our grandmothers' pitchers and armchairs should be considered "objets d'art" and that what is produced in our time, in the same fields, should be nothing but basely utilitarian.' The museum's considerable collection of ceramics by Séraphin Soudbinine (1867–1944) includes his *Lidded Jar* ●, a daring combination of ruggedness and high finish, sculptural form and surface effects. The animal and mineral worlds blend in the matt stoneware fox of the lid handle and in the crackled yellow and brown glaze of the stoneware body. Séraphin Soudbinine's extraordinary, sculptural creations explore the timeless forms of ceramics and archaic bestiaries.

Theatres of dreams

Caught between the two world wars, modernism developed in a decade asphyxiated by the 1929 stock market crash. But not all creative effervescence had disappeared. The blackness of Malraux's *Human Condition* was countered by the dreamlike fantasy of that 'genial jack of all trades' Jean Cocteau, and Christian Bérard, a melancholy painter, brilliant theatre designer and designer of society festivities.

A table by Gilbert Poillerat (1902–88), a friend of Cocteau, has been given pride of place in this evocation of the dreamlike decoration that emerged after the war ● (p. 169).

Poillerat was symptomatic of the return of a certain baroque sensibility. The iconography of the table's base is complex— branches, bucranes, ropes and deer's antlers (made by forge-welding lengths of industrial piping)—on which he placed a stucco imitation-marble top. Cocteau

Soup dish
Jean Emile Puiforcat
Silver, vermeil
1937

Dish
André Thuret
Blown glass, inset decoration, hot-worked
c.1950

Vase
Aristide Colotte
Blown colourless crystal, hot-welded handles,
wheel and burin-engraved
1937

Lidded jar
Séraphin Soudbinine
Glazed stoneware, separate stoneware plinth
c.1933

Vase
Jean Sala
Blown and hot-worked malfin crystal
1948

made ample use of stag's antlers in the sets of his Baroque-Surrealist film *Beauty and the Beast*. *The King and The Queen* ☉ (p. 169) by Janine Janet (1913–2000), who worked with Jean Cocteau, also belong to the same unreal universe. Her fairy-tale figures made of wood and nails were displayed in the windows of the couturier Balenciaga's Paris boutique.

In his innumerable furniture designs, the architect Emilio Terry ☉ borrowed from the same timeless repertoire with disconcerting whimsicality. The fantastic undulations of his *Model of a Spiral House* (1933) contradict the purism of its facades devoid of decoration. The delirious Surrealism of Dali, who painted Terry's portrait, has much in common with these free forms, which breathe a welcome breath of oxygen into modernism. A space is devoted to the plasters in the studio of Alberto (1901–66) and Diego (1902–85) Giacometti.

Alongside his work with his brother, Diego Giacometti developed his own furniture designs, peopling his poetic creations with elongated figures, leaves and comical or serious animals.

Constructing, producing

The problem of the contradictory vocations of man and machine, latent before the war, posed themselves more forcefully in the 1950s ❺❻. The industrial production of artworks was not unrelated to the 'machinism' so criticised by Le Corbusier. He was the first to use the expression 'living machine', in which he believed he could reconcile humanist goals (housing projects) and utilitarian concerns. He saw no conflict between machine and man, between personal fulfilment and 'living units', or between unique pieces and mass production.

These preoccupations were foremost in the mind of Jean Prouvé (1901–84). A space is devoted to his work from the 1930s to the 1950s ☉ (p. 170-171). After learning the craft of wrought-iron as a young man, he soon gave up hand-forging metal to explore new techniques in the workshops he founded at Maxéville near Nancy. His furniture makes abundant use of electric welding and bent sheet metal, which he preferred to the tubing then in fashion. He strove to cater for the specific demands of mass-produced furniture. In 1953–56, he contributed to the Jean-Zay University Hall of Residence at Antony, designing 148 rooms conceived as cells to encourage study.

All of Prouvé's sheet metal and plywood furniture was designed with comfort and economy of means in mind. His tinted wood and painted sheet metal lecturer's or cafeteria table has abrupt architectural lines and its brilliant black evokes the luxury of Art Deco. His subtly curved *Compas* desk (1953) is reduced to the essential: a woodgrain Formica* top and two sets of draws standing on two metallic, compass-shaped legs that seem to be executing a dance step.

Prouvé said that 'to construct a piece of furniture is a very, very serious business if one is designing objects intended for mass-production. Our furniture is subjected to all kinds of mistreatment. It has to withstand so much stress, so many constraints. The problems to resolve are as complex as those of large-scale constructions'. His great achievement was to have reconciled these constraints with elegant forms and the radicalism of his technical solutions.

'Model of a Spiral House'
Emilio Terry
Painted cork, abrasive paper, wood
1933

Table
Gilbert Poillerat
Wrought iron, stucco
1943

'The King' and 'The Queen'
Janine Janet
Wood, nails
1959

p. 170-71
Amphitheatre chair
Cafeteria cloakroom
Lecturer's table
'Antony' low armless chair
'Semi-rest' chair
Jean Prouvé
France 1954–56
Two-armed wall lamp
Serge Mouille
France, 1954

Modern

An open space

The art of living, and living in, the new horizon in the decorative arts in the 1950s, also marked the resolution of a contradiction between interior and exterior. As in Jacques Tati's film *Mon Oncle* (1958), in which the garden and living room are a single continuous space separated merely by a sliding glass door, the modernity of the decorative arts was characterised by a continuity between inside and outside.

The idea of the open-plan interior, and the integration of the exterior into the interior, already well in evidence in the United States, took root in Europe and modified the concept of the living space.

Jean Royère (1902–81), an unclassifiable designer and an enemy of routine and the sectarianism of certain designers, opened the interiors he designed in Cairo, Bagdad, Teheran, Lima and San Paolo onto the exterior. The archives ☞ he donated to Les Arts Décoratifs show the systematic presence of plants, even, in this instance, on the wall hangings. His comfortingly ample *Boule* settee ☞ was a huge success, and his *Liane* lamp ☞ seems to crawl insidiously over the wall. Royère liked to contrast undulating forms with the geometric rigour of a carpet, bare walls, a monumental bed or a winged armchair.

Useful forms

The *Useful Forms, Objects of Our Time* exhibition, organised by the UAM at the Musée des Arts Décoratifs in late 1949, like the annual Salon des Art Ménagers (the French Ideal Home exhibition), which began the following year, showed how

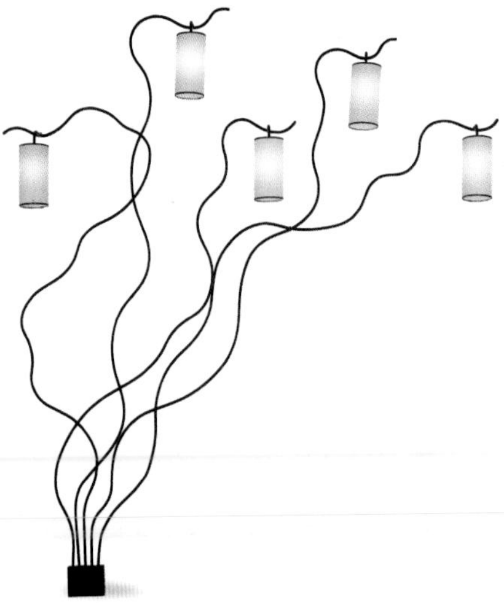

'Liane' lamp
Jean Royère
Patinated iron, Rhodoid
c.1955

Jean Royère

Working for a rich international private clientele, Jean Royère (1902–81) opened design studios all over the world. Distrustful of theories and schools, he was not afraid of saying that the words 'functionalism' and 'contemporary' were meaningless for him. 'That it should be well-executed' was his motto. He began in the import-export business in Le Havre then went to work in a furniture factory.

He was hailed as one of the most innovative designers at the International Exhibition of Arts and Techniques in 1937.

In 1939, in his Eléphanteau armchair, he was the first to experiment with biomorphic forms. In the 1950s, he gave free rein to his 'free forms', using wood, plastic*, perforated sheet metal and, in the apartment of the singer Henri Salvador, fragile straw marquetry.

Design for a drawing room in Bagdad
Jean Royère
Graphite and gouache on Canson paper
1955–60

Boule' or 'Banane' settee
Jean Royère
Wood, foam, wool plush
1947

much contemporary design, in its concern with rationalisation and production techniques, wanted to play an active role in industry.

Charlotte Perriand (1903–99), commissioned with André Hermant to design the UAM's exhibition in 1949, thought nothing of mixing furniture and objects, aircraft propellers and skis...

Unlike the United States, where industrialisation had happened naturally due to the size of the country and its specific needs, few French artists mass-produced their work. There was a notable exception to this, however: Le Corbusier, Pierre Jeanneret and Charlotte Perriand's *L'Equipement intérieur d'une habitation*, manufactured in 1929 by Thonet.

Purity and grace

During this period of reconstruction, Charlotte Perriand insisted on the necessity of the 'harmony of the living space'.

Her bamboo-frame *Chaise longue* ● is a variation on the theme she explored with Le Corbusier and Jeanneret in her legendary *Adjustable chaise longue* in 1928, which set the tone for this new harmony. She discovered bamboo's possibilities during her stay in Japan from 1940. Several pieces, including the *Ombre chair,* evoke the *Synthesis of the Arts* exhibition she organised in Japan in 1946.

Although very purified, her creations always have the same indefinable grace. The Japanese house, light, transparent, opening onto the exterior, with its movable walls and screen, had already confirmed her intui-tions and rejection of clutter in the 1920s. 'It is better to spend a day in the sun than dusting useless objects,' declared the designer who invented the

'storage wall'. The chair, armchair, settee and stool were central concerns of the new generation of designers in the 1950s, perhaps because the chair, which has to reconcile comfort, elegance, solidity and mobility, naturally stimulates the creative imagination.

Joseph-André Motte (born 1925) innovated with an armchair ● whose rattan seat is supported by a cruciform tripod structure held together by a cruciform steel fitting. In the 1900s, winter gardens had been furnished with rattan chairs. Brought back into fashion by Louis Sognot in the 1930s, rattan now perfectly wedded the forms of the body.

Mathieu Matégot (1910–2001) was also fond of this material, which he combined with metal in his little-known *Panamaro* chair in 1952, and his famous *Nagasaki* chair ● around 1950. Pierre Paulin ●(born 1927) had the idea of reducing the chair to three pieces of sewn leather fixed to a stainless steel tubular frame.

Armchair
Pierre Paulin
Stainless steel, leather
Meubles TV
1952

'Tripod' chair
Joseph-André Motte
Rattan, painted steel, beech
1949

'Nagasaki' chair
Mathieu Matégot
Perforated sheet metal and painted steel tubing
c.1950

'Adjustable chaise longue'
Charlotte Perriand
Oak, beech, bamboo
Japan, 1940

The metamorphoses
of the sideboard

The traditional dining-room sideboard also had to comply with the demands of industrial production. Alain Richard (born 1926) lengthened it and veneered it with rosewood ◉: a simple box on six metal legs, but what a lesson in style! The smaller dimensions of the average living space dictated that a piece of furniture now had several uses. An example of this is Antoine Philippon (1930–95) and Jacqueline Lecoq's (born 1932) *TV, record player and drinks cabinet* ◉. Its technical feats were immediately praised and the designers were awarded first prize in the Formica* competition at the Salon des Artistes Décorateurs in 1959. More significantly today, this piece of furniture attests to the contemporary concern for efficiency and economy in the living space. The useful had become utilitarian, but the quest for beauty was still a constant preoccupation.

TV, record player and drinks cabinet
Antoine Philippon and Jacqueline Lecoq
Formica, chrome-plated steel, cherry, polished brass
Prototype
1958–59

Dining-room sideboard
Alain Richard
Rio Rosewood veneer, oak plywood,
painted steel tubing, chrome-plated metal
1958

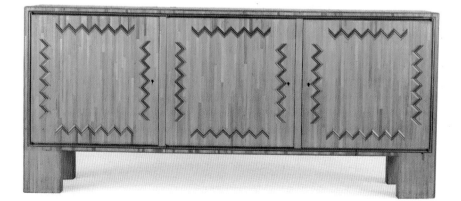

Sideboard
Jean Royère
Wood, straw marquetry
1947

Contemporary The 1960s

saw the increasing standardisation of lifestyles and thought, fuelled by incessant innovations in science and technology. The urbanisation of society and higher standards of living made goods previously reserved by the privileged affordable by all. The miniskirt, pioneered by the English fashion designer Mary Quant in 1965, symbolised youth's liberation from conformism. The dynamism of the young generations was also epitomised by the invasion of new plastics, which transformed everyday objects.

In France, the May 1968 uprising revealed the divergent aspirations of a society shaken by the profound mutations caused by the rapid growth of consumerism and the democratisation of education and culture. It denounced the waste and artificiality of the needs created by constant industrial growth. In *The System of Objects*, the sociologist and philosopher Jean Baudrillard wrote that 'objects tend to form themselves into a coherent system of signs' which structure behaviour.

In the 1980s social problems almost forgotten since the 1930s re-emerged: massive unemployment, the integration of immigrants and inflation. In the United States, thanks to highly active patronage of the arts, artistic production enjoyed a period of major development. Despite the morose economic situation, French cultural life remained very energetic. French presidents concerned with their posterity embarked on large-scale building programmes: the Centre Pompidou, the Musée d'Orsay, the renovation of the Louvre, the Grande Arche, the Opéra-Bastille, the Bibliothèque Nationale de France and the Musée des Arts Premiers. The uniqueness of French culture, which removes cultures from the dictates of international trade, was officially recognised by UNESCO on 20 October 2005.

1967

Soljenitsyn publishes the *Goulag Archipelago*, denouncing Soviet totalitarianism.

1973

Opening of the first Habitat store in France.

1977

Inauguration of the Centre Pompidou.

1989

The fall of the Berlin Wall symbolises the collapse of the USSR and marks the end of the Cold War.

'Tube Chair'
Joe Colombo

Contemporary

The optimism of the Thirties and the unprecedented economic prosperity of the period acted as a locomotive for the decorative arts, fashion and artistic creation in general. The increasing sense of well-being and the development of leisure pursuits went hand in hand with the democratisation of the notion of the art of living.

The newspapers, specialised magazines and even television now revealed the life-styles of stars and prominent personalities. The quest for style affected everyday objects, fuelled by the use of new technologies and new materials such as plastics.

In 1964, Terence Conran opened the first Habitat store in London, selling interior decoration and design at affordable prices. In France, at the instigation of Denise Fayolle and Maïmé Arnaudin, the Prisunic store chain launched a range of cheap design objects designed by some of the most innovative designers of the time. Contemporary design was no longer the privilege of the elite. At the dawn of the do-it-yourself era clients could now choose their own interior decoration. It was the consumer who now had the initiative.

In Georges Perec's novel *Things,* published in 1965, Jérôme and Sylvie, a young middle-class couple, dream of happiness. 'They would have liked to have been rich, [...] Their life would have been an art of living.' But too attached to the things that they acquired, this happiness, tantamount to slavery to objects, proved inaccessible. 'This is because there is an obligatory relationship between the things of modern life and happiness,' Perec wrote. The art of living he evoked refers both to the idea of an aestheticised living space and a certain social status.

Households invested more and more in interior decoration, especially in the United States, where the geographic mobility of families increased the need for a sense of permanence in the home.

The metamorphoses of the chair

On 3 May 1968, while the Latin Quarter was in turmoil, the *Assises du Siège Contemporain* exhibition opened at the Musée des Arts Décoratifs ●. Despite the troubled times, the exhibition was a landmark in what is now called design. The chair was an excellent barometer of new tendencies, and the exhibition revealed many young designers to the general public. On the terraces of a stylised 'mountain', some one hundred chairs arranged chronologically recall this seminal event ❺❼. Among them are several classics such as Harry Bertoïa's *Diamond Chair* ●, designed in New York in 1952 and manufactured by Knoll International. Its diamond-shaped, chrome-plated steel mesh seat, moulded to fit the body, is supported by a bent and welded steel rod frame.

Another design legend is the *670* armchair and footrest ● by Charles (1907–78) and Ray (1912–88) Eames, produced from 1956 and the direct descendent of the comfortable 18th-century *duchesse brisée* armchair. Its tour de force consists in supporting both parts of the chair on a central metal tube acting as a pivot rising from a stable cruciform base. The welcoming curves of its rosewood ply shell, moulded using a newly-perfected tech-nique, the daring combination of metal and wood, and of course its great

'Les Assises du Siège Contemporain'
Saul Steinberg, drawing
Robert Delpire, graphic design
Colour lithograph
1968

'Diamond Chair 421 A'
Harry Bertoïa
Chrome-plated steel mesh, bent steel rod, latex foam
Knoll International
1952

'670' armchair and '671' footrest
Charles and Ray Eames
Moulded rosewood ply, latex, down,
leather, aluminium
Herman Miller
1956

comfort have ensured this adjustable chair's enduring popularity.

Around 1960, the Dane Arne Jacobsen (1902–71) exploited the same formula. His very enveloping moulded polyester armchair and footrest ◉ appear to have been cut out of a giant egg.

In France, Marc Held (born 1932) designed the *Culbuto* series of chairs ◉ using similar ovoid forms. They have a majestically tall back and their round, weighted base enables them to be used as rocking chairs. The *Bulle* armchair ◉, designed by Christian Daninos (1944–92) in 1968, is a perfect hemisphere. Made in Plexiglas mounted on a steel frame, the cocoon-like seat enables all-round visibility while remaining protected inside one's sphere—which also has its own acoustic effects. Its circular mount is echoed by the circular base.

Its radical design is emblematic of the 'futurist' tendency explored by French designers during this revolutionary period. Stanley Kubrick borrowed Olivier Mourgue's furniture for his spacecraft in *2001, a Space Odyssey* (1968).

The Italian Joe Colombo (1930–71) participated in this playful, radical tendency in the 1960s. His *Tube Chair* ◉ is composed of four cylinders fitting into one another.

The lightness of the Pop years

Driven by the enthusiasm for new technologies and stimulated by the sharp rise in purchasing power, especially of adolescents, who could now dictate their own tastes, the lightness of the 'Pop years' inspired the Italian Piero Gatti, Franco Teodoro and Cesare Paolini's *Sacco* chair ◉ (p. 185).

'Egg 3317' armchair and '3127' footrest
Arne Jacobsen
Leather, expanded polyurethane, cast aluminium
Fritz Hansen, 1967
1958

'Culbuto' armchair
Marc Held
Moulded polyester strengthened with fibreglass, plastic foam, fabric
Knoll International, 1970
1967

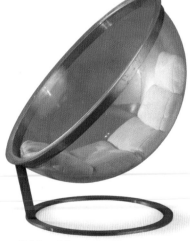

'Bulle' armchair
Christian Daninos
Steel, Plexiglas, fabric
Formes Nouvelles, 1970
1968

'Panton Chair'
Verner Panton
Polyester reinforced with fibreglass
Vitra
1959–60

The reign of plastic

By the time they invaded the world of design in the 1960s, plastics* already had a long industrial history behind them. Ebonite was a by-product of Goodyear's discovery of vulcanisation (hardening rubber by adding sulphur) in 1839. Celluloid did not appear until the end of the century and Bakelite in 1907. In the 1930s, Germany and the United States competed in the development of entirely artifical materials: melamine, Nylon, Plexiglas, polyethylene, etc. With the growth of the petrochemical industry in the 1950s, plastics invaded every aspect of daily life.

In 1959–60, Verner Panton designed the Panton Chair 👁, the first chair made entirely out of plastic. Italian firms such as Kartell, Artemide and Danese pioneered a new aesthetics based on the use of plastics. In France, Quasar produced inflatable furniture. The ability of plastics to imitate organic forms contributed to the abandonment of the rationalist formal vocabulary. Spurred on by the consumer society, plastics espoused the smooth, aloof aesthetics of Pop Art.

'Tube Chair'
Joe Colombo
PVC, metal, rubber, canvas
Flexiform, 1970
1969

Surrealist, provocative and bordering on bad taste, this imitation-leather sack filled with polystyrene beads adapts to the body when one sits on it. It was a huge commercial success. It perfectly reflected the freedom of the new lifestyle and its liberalisation of postures: one could have a nap, read a paperback or smoke in it. Another sign of this newfound freedom was the concept of an open-plan living space that Pierre Paulin and Olivier Mourgue were developing at that time, furnished with thick foam rubber carpets so that one could live 'on the floor'. In interior decoration too, everything was now possible and permissible.

In this context it was hardly surprising that designers became interested in children's furniture. A section is devoted to it, including Marco Zanuso and Richard Sapper's indefatigable and vividly coloured little stacking chairs ◉.

Design enters the kitchen

The fashionable living room, the designer bookshelf, the fitted kitchen... Attitudes changed. In the open-plan interiors dear to the modernists, the kitchen was seamlessly integrated into the living room. The days of the sacrosanct dining room, inherited from the 19th century, were numbered. The design of all objects, from the refrigerator to the teaspoon, changed radically.

In 1970, the seminal *A table* exhibition at the Musée des Arts Décoratifs unveiled new approaches to tableware. Roger Tallon (born 1929) showed his *3T* service ◉, one of the most original pieces. A silversmith, a porcelain manufacturer and a glassmaker collaborated in the making of this complete service

designed by Tallon. He wanted to produce it in materials ranging from crystal* to plastic* but only the luxury version was produced as a complete service. The cutlery was manufactured, however, in silver-plated steel and stainless steel, and its purified forms and ergonometric forms proved quite popular.

Modular aesthetics also developed in tableware, dictated by the size of the European home which, unlike American living spaces, diminished in size after the war. Furniture and objects now had to be functional and light but also adaptable and flexible. Like chairs, which were increasingly systematically stackable, more and more objects adopted the same principles.

The plates and cups of Helen von Boch's *La Bomba* picnic service ◉ fit into one another to form an easily transportable and storable cylinder. Saara Hopea-Untracht's *Stackable glasses* ◉ are also symptomatic of the new obsession with saving space. Coloured and perfectly adapted to the spatial constraints of cupboards, they have been a perennial bestseller. One practical constraint was resistance to machine washing. In 1960, Ulla Procopé's *Ruska* table service, one of the Scandinavian firm Arabia's most famous, was one of the first to be both oven and dishwasher-proof.

Contrasting with these mass-produced objects, a selection of glass and ceramics dating from the 1950s to the 1990s ⑤⑧ shows the vitality of hand-crafted artistic creations. This display refers to two exhibitions, *Céramique française contemporaine, sources et courants*, in 1981, and *Verriers français contemporains: art et industrie*, in 1982. Although figuration is present in Jacqueline and Jean Lerat's stoneware* *Anthropomorphic*

'Sacco'
Piero Gatti, Cesare Paolini, Franco Teodoro
Polystyrene, imitation leather
Zanotta, 1990
1968–69

'La Bomba' picnic service
Helen von Boch
Villeroy & Boch
Melamine, steel, stainless steel
c.1975

'3T' service
Roger Tallon
Glazed porcelain, brushed stainless steel, blown crystal
1967–69

'K 1340' children's chairs
Marco Zanuso, Richard Sapper
Injection-moulded polyethylene
Kartell, 1963
1960

Stackable glasses and water jug
Saara Hopea-Untracht
Nuutajärvi glassworks
Blow-moulded glass
1954

Contemporary

Vase ⊙, reminiscent of the powerful pre-historic Venuses, and the glazed faience by Jean Lurçat ⊙ (p. 187), Suzanne Ramié ⊙ and Pablo Picasso, the abstract forms of the creations of Philippe Lambercy, Elisabeth Joulia and Robert Deblander seem dictated by the material itself.

Internationally famous designers—Tapio Wirkkala, Roberto Sambonet, Ettore Sottsass—now produced works for major glass manufacturers such as Daum, Venini and Baccarat. Glass was transformed into sculpture by César, Gilioli and the German artist Jutta Cuny, who sandblasted indus-trial glass. Alongside the international community of independent glassmakers, ranging from Richard Meitner to Toots Zynsky ⊙, Dale Chihuly and Libensky-Brychtova, the French excelled with Claude and Isabelle Monod, Alain and Marysa Bégou. Trained by their grandfa-ther, the great François Décorchemont, Antoine and Etienne Leperlier subjected glass paste to new techniques such as the use of plastic moulds. In the North Room, a montage of publicity films advertising design obejcts will immerse you in the creative melting pot of the 1960s and 70s. By integrating design into the home, the consumer could now create his own style. Individualist behaviour now went hand in hand with individualist taste.

The democratisation of design, whose forms were now increasingly diverse, rang the death knell of moderation. Sitting at the entrance to the room like temple guardians, Ruth Francken's *Man chair* ⊙, a headless plastic cast, and Roger Tallon's *Portrait of Caesar* chair add an ironic touch to the universe of design. They contrast with the twisted neon lamps by Atelier A, created by François Arnal, Robert Malaval and Arman among others.

Milan, New York, Tokyo

As an introduction to the spectacular mutations which changed the design scene in the 1980s and 90s, a room is devoted to some of the 'giants' who left their mark on international creation ㊾. Alessandro Mendini, who was born in Milan in 1931, and trained as an archi-tect, was one of the advocates of the *Neomodernismo* which revolutionised Italian design. He was an influential theorist and a deliberately irreverent and ironic designer who juggled with past and present styles. His famous *Proust* arm-chair ⊙ reproduces the worst excesses of 19th-century bourgeois furniture, which was in turn influenced by the art of the previous century. An outrageous pseudo-Pointillist painting covers the entire chair, wood and fabric alike. At the height of Postmodernism, architects and designers pillaged the styles of the past and rein-terpreted them in a deliberately subjec-tive manner. Around Mendini's armchair are arranged a series of identical vases decorated at his invitation by a variety of artists.

Another major figure of the period, Ettore Sottsass (born 1917), also helped liberate the young generation from the rationalism inherited from Le Corbusier, which was still the basis of architectural education in the early 1960s. 'When I was young,' declared this son of an architect, 'all anyone ever talked about was functionalism, functionalism, func-tionalism. It wasn't enough. Design also had to be sensual, exciting.' In 1981, he founded the Memphis collective, which included the designers Andrea Branzi, Matteo Thun, Nathalie du Pasquier and Michele De Lucchi. Experimenting with vivid colours, cheap materials and kitsch

'Anthropomorphic Vase'
Jean and Jacqueline Lerat
Stoneware
1974

'Blue moon total eclipse Isla Bella'
Toots Zynsky
Hot-worked amalgamated glass thread
1987

'Baroque Vase'
Jean Lurçat
Sant Vicens pottery
Glazed faience
Perpignan, c.1960

Tripod vase
Suzanne Ramié
Atelier Madoura
Glazed faience
Vallauris, 1950

'Poltrona di Proust' armchair
Alessandro Mendini
Wood, fabric, acrylic paint
Studio Alchimia
Italy, 1979

'Man' chair
Ruth Francken
Polyurethane foam, polished stainless steel
Gallery X Plus
1985

motifs, Sottsass also brilliantly used age-old materials such as glass, producing original forms, as demonstrated here by a work produced at the Centre International de Recherche sur le Verre (CIRVA) ●.

As design increasingly saw itself as an ephemeral art, as an art of adaptation and flexibility, it also became increasingly liable to go out of fashion. It was this phenomenon, which emerged in the 60s, that sealed the break with the modern period, whose standard bearers had advocated the values of permanence, continuity and the integrity of materials.

The Italian Gaetano Pesce, based in New York since 1980, was just as radical as Sottsass in his optimist exploitation of synthetic materials and colours. His moulded polyester *Sansone* table ● appears to be tottering on its four legs of different diameter. This technical tour de force illustrates the hand-crafted aspect of his work. This emphasis on the mastery of techniques is typical of the 'new design', which deliberately gravitated towards the production of expensive pieces and limited editions. The chairs from the *Dalila* series arranged around it have the same expressive plasticity. Like chrysalises, they seem to be caught in a straight jacket in which mysterious transmutations are taking place.

The stacking of the more overtly organic forms of Andrea Branzi's blown glass 'liana' vases seem to bring them alive. One of the most important theorists of the 'new design', Branzi (born 1938) epitomised its radical tendency and opened the way for the Neoprimitivist creations of the 1980s.

Fascinated by western culture and influenced by the work of Marcel Duchamp and the American Minimalists, the Japanese designer Shiro Kuramata (1934–91) often exhibited with the Minimalists in Europe and the United States and joined the Memphis group in 1981. His purified designs, at the frontier of art and design, are profoundly anchored in Japanese culture, in which the notion of art emerged relatively late, influenced by the West. The lightness of the falling feathers inside his *Acrylic Stool* ●, designed in 1990, contrasts with the mass of the block in which they are imprisoned. The stool's transparency evokes the emptiness of the domestic spaces of the traditional Japanese house, in which one sits on the floor. Both evanescent and monumental, it is above all a sculpture.

Parisian audacities

The space devoted to French design in the 1980s and 90s highlights several very diverse personalities ㉑. Freed from functionalism by the postmodernists and influenced by the vitality of the Italians, especially by Mendini and Sottsass, French designers returned to the tradition of 'fine craftsmanship' and the 'decorative' but also explored the purely formal properties of everyday objects. Yet a gulf separated the dishevelled creations of Garouste and Bonetti, who claimed to be anti-design and anti-mass-production, and the minimalist creations of François Bauchet and Martin Szekely. The universe of each of these designers is evoked in a 'box' on wheels.

In 1987, Elisabeth Garouste (born 1946) and Mattia Bonetti (born 1952) decorated the salons of Christian Lacroix's couture house. The walls were painted in warm colours and the light-coloured curtains were bordered with black velvet, whose tattered outline created a setting for the

Glass, 'Lingam' series
Ettore Sottsass
Blown glass
CIRVA, Marseille
Netherlands, 2000

'Acrylic Stool with Feathers'
Shiro Kuramata
Acrylic, aluminium, feathers
Ishimaru Co
1990

'Sansone' table
Gaetano Pesce
Moulded polyester resin
Cassina
1980
Podium made by the artist, 2006

whimsical furniture. This theatrical and joyous universe was inspired by Emilio Terry and the great interior designers of the 1940s. Garouste and Bonetti willingly acknowledged their sources, 'from the Middle Ages to Africa with a touch of Cocteau's poetry and Venetian baroque...'. The *Rocher* low table, the *Prince impérial* chair ◉ and the *Enfer* cabinet illustrate range of their talent.

The more austere space dedicated to Philippe Starck (born 1949) introduces you to the universe of the enfant terrible of French design. This prolific designer has put his hand to everything from the toothbrush to the private apartments in the Elysée Palace (1982) and pasta. An object must first of all 'give the help we ask of it'. The designer also dreamt that the user could develop an 'affectionate bond' with the object. The *Dr Bloodmoney* folding armchair (1979) and *Lola Mundo* chair-table ◉ (p. 195) are examples of his style, whose audacity is always tempered with warm familiarity.

Olivier Gagnère (born 1952) is represented by an ensemble evoking another famous Paris café, the Café Marly ◉. His classically shaped, velvet upholstered chairs and languidly curved Murano chandeliers recreate the atmosphere of a boudoir in the heart of the Louvre. His *Bench* (1983), uses an unusual combination of lemonwood, aluminium and ceramics, which Gagnère has used regularly in France (Limoges, Vallauris, etc.) and also in Japan and China.

With his *Pi* series ◉ of chairs and small furniture, Martin Szekely (born 1956), who trained first as a graphic designer then as a cabinetmaker, combined Zen rigour with masterful use of angular lines and welcoming curves. As it had done with Philippe Starck in 1982, VIA (Association pour la valorisation de l'innovation dans l'ameublement) gave Martin Szekely carte blanche to produce a piece of furniture. The result was the *Pi* chaise longue, one of the symbols of the 1980s, then the whole *Pi* collection.

Due to the Japanese influence, black was always in fashion. It defined an object's outline, projecting into space an uncompromising geometry with the organic forms of the 1960s and 70s. Philippe Starck's *Tertio* furniture, designed at the same time for the Trois Suisses mail order firm, was also gloss black.

François Bauchet (born 1948), who trained as a sculptor, works in solid materials. His *This is also a chair* chair ◉ (p. 192), designed in 1992, appears to have been carved out of a block of concrete, but is in fact made of plywood and therefore light and hollow. Despite its small size, its monumental forms give it great authority. The pieces by Sylvain Dubuisson (born 1946) evoke the furniture commissioned in 1990 for the office of the Culture Minister. Dubuisson adapted his famous *Bureau 1989* ◉ (p. 193), shown the year before at an exhibition organised by VIA at the Musée des Art Décoratifs, amplifying its curves. Its rounded form, emphasised by the parchment-veneered top, reminds one of the spiral of a seashell. An architect, and influenced as much by literature as mathematics, Dubuisson imbues all his designs with his own personal poetry, whether in prestige commissions of industrially produced pieces.

'Prince impérial' chair
Elisabeth Garouste, Mattea Bonetti
Painted wood and branches, raphia
Neotu
1985

'Mine' vase
Bench
'Café Marly' armchair
'Caigo Collection' chandelier
Olivier Gagnère
1983–2002

'Carbone' chair, 'Pi' collection
Martin Szekely
Carbon fibre, painted steel
Tribu
Paris, 1983

Very High Speed design

The decades from 1960 to 2000 were marked by numerous technological advances and the ever-closer relationship between industrial design and high-tech. Roger Tallon played a major role in the commitment of designers to technology ❻. An internationally respected industrial designer, he designed the Mexico City Metro in 1969 and the Corail railway carriages for the SNCF four years later.

This revolution in transportation would be developed in his work on the TGV Atlantique (1983), Eurostar (1991) and the TGV Duplex (1996), the most accomplished in his view 👁 (p. 194). The space devoted to him emphasises the industrial aspect of his work. As the *CAD for the mega TGV* shows, the TGV was the first generation of rolling stock to be designed using computer-assisted design (CAD). In his 'high-speed' projects, Tallon endeavoured, in his own words, 'to forget railway archaisms and work for the mutation of railway transport by discovering all aspects of what will become the most important form of mass transit in the future'.

'This is also a chair'
François Bauchet
Painted plywood
Neotu
1982

'L' lamp
Sylvain Dubuisson
Sèvres porcelain, feathers, crystal beads
Sèvres national manufactory, 1990

The minister's office

François Mitterrand's election to the French presidency in 1981, apart from the major building projects which modified the Parisian architectural landscape, also brought design into some of the national palaces. In the Elysée Palace, Marc Held, Annie Tribel, Roland Cecil Sportes, Philippe Starck and Jean-Michel Wilmotte refurbished the private apartments, and Pierre Paulin designed the new furniture for the president's office. The Finance Minister's office at Bercy was designed by Andrée Putman, who also designed the furniture for the Culture Minister's office in the Palais-Royal in 1985. Five years later, Sylvain Dubuisson was commissioned to design new furniture for this office. The desk and chairs, made in the workshops of the Mobilier National, are in honey-coloured lourofaya wood and ivory-coloured leather. The desk is a variation of his 1989 desk, which the minister, Jack Lang had admired. He amplified its curves for the Palais-Royal office, and the chair, placed laterally in the original design, returned to its traditional central place. The armchairs, whose spiral metal wire legs contained symbolic objects in the 1989 version, have a more classic base evoking the solidity of Empire and Restauration furniture. The wool carpet, made at the Savonnerie manufactory, has geometric perspective tile pattern.

Design for the desk of the Culture Minister
Sylvain Dubuisson
Pencil and coloured pencil
1990

'1989' desk, 'Apartment' model
Sylvain Dubuisson
Lourofaya wood veneered with parchment, leather
Fourniture
1991

The international scene ⑥

Born in Australia in 1963, Marc Newson made his name with a riveted aluminium chaise longue with rounded, lazy forms (1986–88). His *Pod of Drawers* 👁 belongs to this vein of metal-sheathed furniture conveying his passion for the two fields he later worked in, automobile design and aviation. The portliness of this chest of drawers evokes one of the most famous pieces in the Arts Décoratifs' collection, André Groult's *Anthropomorphic Chiffonnier,* designed in 1925 (see p. 146). Newson's title for the work alludes to the colloquial expression, 'to be in pod,' ('to have a bun in the oven').

1st-class TGV chair for the TGV Duplex
Roger Tallon
Aluminium alloy, jersey velvet
1998

Equally fascinated by the brilliance of polished metal, Ron Arad (born 1951) combines his playful exploration of forms with the most cutting-edge technology. His *Parpadelle* chair 👁 (p. 197) is made from a length of stainless steel chain mail unrolled like a carpet, which suddenly freezes into the form of a chair.

Due to his international reputation, Philippe Starck, is also present in this space. His *Richard III* chair (1984), when viewed from the front, has the ample forms of a traditional leather club chair, but in profile it reveals its hollow structure and simple moulded plastic shell. His *W.W. Stool* 👁, designed for the filmmaker Wim Wenders, looks like some strange creature, half-bird half-plant, with gentle purified curves.

Compared to this universe, in which one plays with forms as one does words, the work of Jasper Morrison (born 1959), seems all the more ascetic. His *Ply chair Open* was shown in an installation in the seminal *Some New Items for the House* exhibition in Berlin in 1988. In it, Morrison explores the familiar, even banal forms of

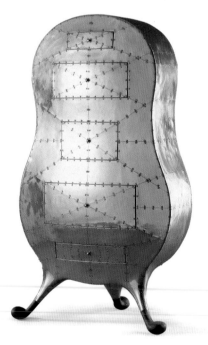

'Pod of Drawers'
Marc Newson
Sheet aluminium, wood, fibreglass
Made 1997, 1999

'A Strange Thing Against a Wall' vase
Philippe Starck
Blown crystal, industrial glass
Daum
1988

Philippe Starck

Like a meteorite that had landed in the French design scene, Philippe Starck started his first company in 1968. He began by making inflatable objects. In the late 1970s, he decorated two Parisian nightclubs, La Main Bleue and Les Bains-Douches. In 1979, he formed Starck Products and developed a line of industrialised objects. His famous Richard III *chair, dated 1984, is one of the pieces he designed for the private apartments of the Elysée Palace, which he was then decorating. Similarly, he produced a highly successful tripod chair for the Café Costes (demolished 1984), whose interior he also designed. Now in orbit on the international scene, he designed hotels and restaurants in Tokyo, New York, Hong Kong and Mexico City. His passion for industrial design led him to rethink everyday objects from the toothbrush to the motorscooter, and even the Olympic flame. His easily recognisable style, influenced at the outset by Memphis and post-modern aesthetics, has evolved towards purified organic forms.*

'W.W. Stool'
Philippe Starck
Moulded and lacquered aluminium
Vitra
1990

'Lola Mundo' chair-table
Philippe Starck
Tinted multipli, cast aluminium, rubber
Driade
1986

the most elementary furniture. But when one looks closer one notices the subtle 'corrections' he made to obtain its quintessential form.

A display of glass, ceramics and precious metalware entitled *The Object Laboratory* ❻ illustrates the experimental role of these creations, some of which were state commissions. Traditional materials are subjected to novel constraints. The British artist Ursula Morley-Price, in her *Japanese Flange,* succeeds in transforming porcelaineous stoneware into the evanescent forms of some gorgonia or jellyfish. In *Meules vives* 👁, Bernard Dejonghe combines the infinite delicateness of foliage and mineral coarseness.

Nomadism

In the 1960s, influenced by the tatamis and the carpets of the traditional Japanese house and the tents of nomadic peoples, many designers brought the living space down to floor level, where seats, floor coverings and wall hangings could blend. This type of open habitat, freed of social conventions, symbolised the new relaxed and convivial lifestyle. The young designers of the late 1990s were in turn seduced by the idea of designing spaces with multi-purpose structures, if necessary overturning the traditional uses of pieces of furniture. The space devoted to them in museum will constantly evolve to reflect current trends ❻.

A sign of the times was the replacement of the triumphant optimism of the 1960s by a sense of nomadism, even precariousness. Matali Crasset's (born 1965) *When Jim goes up to Paris* 👁, enables its owner to transform any space into an ephemeral room. Rather than clutter a cupboard, the

foam mat and mattress, when rolled up, form a kind of stele that can be stood in the corner of a room. An alarm clock and a portable, lantern-shaped bedside lamp add a note of intimacy to this deliberately austere ensemble. With this piece, designed in 1995, Matali Crasset expressed for the first time her highly personal approach to design. Instead of the cult of the beautiful solitary object, it is gestures, mobility and space which count.

Like all children, the Bouroullec brothers, Ronan (born 1971) and Erwan (born 1976), liked to build cabins. They continued as adults to dream of these protective shelters. In 2000, they attracted attention with their *Box Bed,* a kind of cabin on stilts recreating the intimate space of one of the emblematic pieces of furniture of their native Britanny. Their *Cabin* 👁 (p. 198–99) fulfills the same need for a protective structure, but the private space encapsulated by its large metallic cloth-covered hoops remains open to the surrounding environment.

With his *Diana* series of tables and *Chair One* 👁 (p. 201), the German designer Konstantin Grcic (born 1965) created a visual alphabet whose elements can be recombined at will. These small pieces of furniture, simple assemblages of sheet metal evoking the strict geometry of Russian Constructivism, reveal a subtle sense of humour. An unexpectedly precarious balance here, and an incongruous slanting plane there, seem to echo each other from one piece to another.

The diversity of these creations is symptomatic of a new tendency towards sobriety and bareness in reaction to the joyous cacophony of Memphis and the deliberately kitsch optimism of certain designs in the 1980s. In the work of the Droog

'When Jim goes up to Paris' bed
Matali Crasset
Foam, felt
Domeau & Pérès
1995

'Meules vives'
Bernard Dejonghe
Moulded optical glass,
partially devitrified, polished grindstone
1995

'The Japanese Flange'
Ursula Morley-Price
Porcelaineous stoneware
United Kingdom, 1992

'Parpadelle' chair
Ron Arad
Stainless steel chain mail, polished steel
One Off Ltd
1992

Design collective, founded in Amsterdam in 1993, this return to rigour began to look like a revolt. Tejo Remy's *You can't lay down your memories* chest of drawers ● is both a critique of consumer society and the waste it generates and an ironic reflection on memory. A precarious-looking bundle of old drawers, it is 'as chaotic' as the memories stored any-old-how in our brain—the Dutch word *droog* means a type of disenchanted humour.

.

'You can't lay down your memories' chest of drawers
Tejo Remy
Second-hand drawers, maple, cord
Droog Design
1991

'Chair One'
Konstantin Grcic
Painted aluminium, varnished concrete
Magis
2003

'Sushi'
Fernando and Umberto Campana
Fabric, felt
Edra
2002

Toy Gallery

When the young child plays it is miming the gestures of everyday life. Later, it gives these fictitious beings imaginary lives. Toys reflect this universe of illusion and wonder, and down the centuries they have mirrored our daily lives.

Doll's clothes follow the fashion of the moment, doll's houses are furnished in the style of the time. All toys, from the humble rattle to the electronic game, tell us about the children of yesteryear and today and their play practices. Toys retrace the history of a society and its evolution, and attest to economic fluctuations and the evolution of techniques and materials. Toys echo scientific discoveries and the great moments of history. They can be made by artisans or designers, manufactured by small, traditional firms or industrially produced.

For all these reasons, toys naturally have their place in the Musée des Arts Décoratifs. Dolls, doll's houses and their furniture, teddy bears, cars, boats, planes, robots, figurines, board games and animated toys take us back our own childhood and transport us again into its imaginary worlds.

The museum's collection of some 12,000 toys, ranges from Frozen Charlie to Felix the Cat, Becassine, the Nautilus, Pinocchio, Apollo II, Darth Vador, Harry Potter, the expeditions to the Poles, Noah's Ark, and of course mechanical toys. Some date back to before the French Revolution, but most were made after 1870. After the Second World War, the European market opened up to American and Japanese imports. The main toy manufacturers today are in China, which now produces 90% of the world's toys.

The collection began in 1905 with the opening of the Musée des Arts Décoratifs in the Louvre and the founding of the Société des Amateurs de Jouets et Jeux Anciens, a group of collectors of antique toys and games interested in the aesthetic education of children. Its successive presidents were the journalist Léo Claretie and the historian Henry-René D'Allemagne, two great collectors whose publications are still standard reference works on the history of French toys. The example this society set was decisive in the development of the museum's historic toy collection. However, it was not until 1975 that a fully-fledged Toy Department was created within the museum. The collection developed from then on with some 20 thematic

Teddy bear
Steiff
Mohair, wood shavings, glass, embroidery, felt
Germany, 1922

Frog on a tricycle
Unpainted and painted wood
France, c.1930

'Frozen Charlie'
Painted porcelain, knitted costume
Germany, c.1880

Air France 541 Croix du Sud
Joustra
Clockwork toy, lithographed metal
France, 1954

Toy Gallery

exhibitions. The most important of these were, *American Small Children's Toys* in 1977–78, *Large Exhibition of French Toys* in 1982–83, *The Circus and the Toy* in 1984–85, *Wooden Toys From all Countries* in 1987–88, *Teddy Bear Stories* in 1994, *Yesterday's Dolls, Today's Creations* in 1991, and *Toytown* in 1996–97.

The Toy Gallery, in the museum's south wing, was designed by the architect Bernard Desmoulins. The presentations in the display cases are renewed twice yearly. The collection is arranged historically and thematically, with 'carte blanches' given to contemporary designers. In the multimedia room regularly changed films and video games, etc., can be viewed and sampled by the public.

The aim of these presentations is to view toys in different lights and to enrich our vision of them with contemporary approaches.

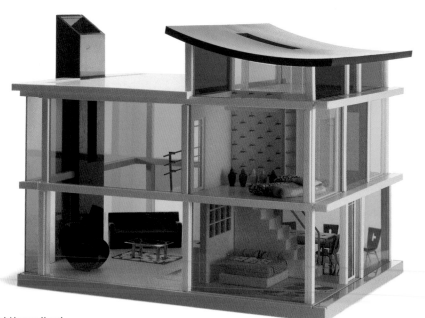

'Kaleidoscope House'
Laurie Simmons and Peter Wheelwright, designers
Bozart
Plastic and miscellaneous materials
United States, 2001

Wage Uglydoll
David Horvath and Kim Sun-Min, designers
Prettyugly LLC
Polyester fibre plush, silvery black fabric
United States, 2003

Robot W
Noguchi
Clockwork mechanism, printed metal and plastic
Japan, c.1965

Girl doll
Georges Lepage
Painted and varnished wood, fabric, blond mohair,
wood, cotton, black imitation leather
France, 1916

Dubuffet Gallery

Jean Dubuffet (1901–85) did not like museums, those 'morgues of embalmment' which ensure that 'the creation of art will always be antagonist to culture'. The donation he made to the museum in 1967 could therefore seem surprising. But if he appeared to put his principles to one side, this was due to his friendship with the museum's head curator, François Mathey.

The 132 drawings and gouaches, 400 lithographs, 21 paintings and 6 sculptures enable us to follow his artistic development from the post-war years to *The Hourloupe* series. Dubuffet was making a statement by donating these works to a museum of decorative arts rather than a museum of modern art. He was saying that they were not destined for an elite public but to be 'used'. From 1947 to 1951, he drew almost like a child. *Portrait of Jean Paulhan* (1945) and *Jouhandeau with Glasses* perfectly illustrate his key idea that 'if I paint a hollow path, I want it to be an archetype of the hollow path of the world'. Instead of reproducing a face's characteristic features, his portraits depersonalise each model into a 'human effigy'. From 1949, in exhibitions of Art Brut, he unveiled not his sources but at least the authentically naïve mode of expression he had chosen: the art of children, the mentally deranged and graffiti. He used materials considered unworthy such as cinders, grease and gravel. In *Theatre of the Desert,* he showed his fascination for sand, in which all imprints and footsteps mingle and disappear, each time composing a new palimpsest.

He then turned to assemblage in pictures and sculptures using raw animal and vegetable materials, then to manifestations of decrepitude such as rust and the pulverulence of old walls. In the late 1950s, he began his *Texturologies*, a 'celebration of the ground' which he regarded as a vast illegible scrawl. *Hôtel du Cantal* (1961) and *Rue de Passy (Lèche dodo)*, painted in 1962, marked his return to the human figure in naïve and coloured pictures. In 1962, with the *Hourloupe* series, he explored a new, falsely rational language, emphasising forms with black outlines and hatched surfaces and decomposing the human figure into a multicoloured, absurd jigsaw puzzle.

'The Lost Donkey'
Jean Dubuffet
Botanic elements and gouache on paper
France, 1959

'Affaires en ville'
Jean Dubuffet
Oil on canvas
France, 1962

'Chameau bourlingue EG 69'
Jean Dubuffet
Gouache on paper
France, 1963

Jewellery Gallery

The origins of jewellery are lost in the mists of time, as are those of decorative art, of which it was one of the first manifestations. Jewellery was the privilege of the warrior before it became that of woman. The Musée des Arts Décoratifs has the largest collection of jewellery in the French national collections: over 4,000 pieces dating from Antiquity to the present day.

The 1,200 pieces on display in the Jewellery Gallery trace the history of finery from the Middle Ages to contemporary times.

One of the most ancient pieces is a gold ring dating from the Merovingian period (perhaps the 5th century) with rays inset with garnets. Another major piece dating from ancient times is a Byzantine gold ring engraved with a Virgin and Child in majesty.

For several centuries, jewellery was decorated mainly with religious motifs and subjects. A 16th-century French gold pendant depicts the Mystic Lamb, whose body is formed by a baroque* pearl. This type of pearl, extremely fashionable during in the Renaissance, was often used for court jewellery all over Europe. The 17th century is represented by numerous pendants, above all from Spain. They vary in form—jigsawed or heart-shaped—and are set in an openwork gold frame and sometimes decorated with enamel of small baroque pearls. The central cameo is underglass-painted, usually with religious scenes.

But female jewellery would soon eclipse devotional finery. The museum has a magnificent collection of bodice ornaments 👁, which were originally sewn to the dress. They are composed of floral motifs in silver or gold inset with diamonds and coloured precious stones such as emeralds, aquamarines and rubies. They continued to be fashionable in the 18th century. The most spectacular was made in Spain. Its three elements are crowned by an eagle and it weds the rounded form of the bodice.

With the period of prosperity during the century of the Enlightenment, the diamond, hitherto reserved for the powerful, became more widespread. The Neoclassical style which emerged in the late 18th century prompted a desire to unify the parure: the necklace, earrings, comb and broach were now often decorated with the same motif and precious stones. Each of the pieces of a parure

Sphinx watch and chatelaine
Alphonse Fouquet
Chased gold
Paris, 1878

Bracelet
Alphonse Fouquet, designer
Albert-Ernest Carrier-Belleuse, sculptor
Honoré (known as Honoré Bordoncle), chaser
Paul Grandhomme, enameller
Chased gold (several tones), painted enamel on gold,
rose-cut diamonds
France, 1883

Bodice ornament
Silver and chrysoberyls
France, 18th century

Cross of the Order of Christ
Silver gilt, topaz, garnet?
Portugal, 18th century

Comb
Matt gold, tortoiseshell, carnelian, pearls, enamel
France, First Empire (1804–14)

Jewellery Gallery

dating from the Empire period ● (p. 209) is decorated with the same combination of gold, carnelian and pearls. Antique motifs such as cameos, amphorae and Greek fret* remained fashionable for most of the 19th century, while Ancient Egyptian motifs added an exotic, mysterious note. Two new techniques gave early 19th-century jewellery a new brilliance: graineti (gold grains welded together) and purl (gold or silver wire thread). The revival in interest in France's artistic heritage caused certain pieces made from the 1820s to the 1840s to look like miniature Gothic hunts. The composite style of the Second Empire and the 1880s borrowed both from the Renaissance and the 18th century. The taste for technical excellence went in hand in hand with the rediscovery of ancient techniques such as painted enamel, illustrated by the sumptuous bracelet by Alphonse Fouquet ● (p. 209), with a bust of Diana. Art Nouveau, influenced by Japonism, swept historicism to one side, replacing it with motifs from nature: realistically depicted leaves, foliage, flowers, insects and small animals. Woman, serpentine and enigmatic, was a major source of inspiration. Precious materials were now used with horn, glass paste, ivory*, crystal* and stones such as moonstone. René Lalique ●, hailed as the inventor of modern jewellery, is represented by a magnificent ensemble. The jewellery he created for the famous American heiress Natalie Clifford Barney, is decorated with a flight of bats. In the 1920s, Art Deco marked a return to strict geo-metry and previously rarely used materials such as platinum, onyx, coral, lacquered silver and engraved glass. Like Jean Després, Raymond Templier explored the harsh forms of machinism, transposing them into stylised, very pure forms. In the 1950s and 60s, artists such as Georges Braque and Jean Lurçat created veritable miniature sculptures, and Alexander Calder ● recreated the fragile universe of his mobiles in pieces in hammered silver. The great tradition of French luxury jewellery is also represented by pieces by Jean Schlumberger, who began by designing jewellery for Schiaparelli. The contemporary era marked a veritable revolution: jewellery could now be made in humble materials such as aluminium, acrylic and even photographic film. Certain creations, such as Jacomijn der Donk's daring *Hands* ●, are almost pieces of clothing and renew the 17th-century tradition of the bodice ornament.

'Mistletoe' comb
Paul and Henri Vever
Gold, tortoiseshell, pearl, enamel
France, 1900

Broach
Alexander Calder
Silver
France, c.1955

'Kiss' broach
René Lalique
Patinated and chased silver, moulded and patinated glass
France, c.1904–06

'Hands' necklace
Jacomijn Van der Donk
Oxidised silver lace
Netherlands, 1994

Prints and Drawings

The Prints and Drawings Department's collection of over 100,000 drawings, albums and sketchbooks is extraordinary in its encyclopaedic range: from the work of an anonymous 15th-century ornamentalists to sketches by Rodin for *The Gates of Hell* ◉ (p. 214). The collection was born out of the will of the founders of what would become the Musée des Arts Décoratifs to make the finest examples of past and contemporary creation available to artists and artisans.

Drawings play a crucial didactic role as the indispensable counterpart to the furniture and objects in the museum. Some drawings were mounted in the albums in the library and classified by theme. To meet modern conservation standards, they have been transferred to a special store-room. They are now shown on a rotary basis in certain spaces in the museum to illustrate themes related to the surrounding works. They can also be viewed by appointment in the department's consultation room.

Entirely logically, drawings of ornaments are well in evidence, as is their obligatory corollary, the architectural drawing. Both mingle in the drawings of Charles Lebrun, the grand coordinator of the pomp of Louis XIV, and also the exceptional group of works bequeathed by Emilio Terry (1890–1969). An architect and a friend of Salvador Dali, Terry drew on 18th-century forms in his whimsical, poetic compositions ◉ (p. 215). Another singular interior designer and designer, but one less prone to nostalgia, Jean Royère (1902–81), is brilliantly represented by the archives he donated to Les Arts Décoratifs.

The eclectic decoration of the Second Empire is present in numerous furniture designs but also in depictions of some of the most famous residences of the time: the painter Eugène Lami's watercoloured drawings for his decorations in the Château de Ferrières, for example. Garden design, notably with the important Duchesne Collection, and the world of the theatre (costume designs created by Bosquet around 1780, gouaches by Léon Bakst for Diaghilev's Ballets Russes).

The models for Sonia Delaunay's *Tissus Simultanés* ◉ (p. 215) rub shoulders with drawings by Pierre-Victor Galland for teaching the decorative arts. The department

**Design for a candelabrum
with five bras de lumière for Louis XV**
Juste-Aurèle Meissonnier
Pen and black ink, grey and yellow wash
and white highlighting on a pencil sketch on paper
France, 1739

'Portrait of Charles Lethière as a Child'
Jean Dominique Ingres
Graphite on paper
Rome, 1818

Two desk designs
Giroux album
Gouache
France, Second Empire (1852–70)

**The letter Y,
for the 'Larousse pour tous'
encyclopaedia**
Eugène Grasset
Pencil, pen and black ink on tracing paper
France, late 19th century

Prints and Drawings

also has the alphabet Eugène Grasset designed for that early 20th-century monument, the *Larousse pour tous* encyclopaedia ◉ (p. 213).

Precious metalwork and jewellery are of course also present with priceless works by Alphonse Fouquet, Raymond Templier and Jean Schlumberger. The collection also includes designs for stained glass, ceramics, Japanese prints and several masterpieces from outside the domain of the decorative arts: a red chalk drawing by Antoine Watteau, charcoals by Edgard Degas, *Portrait of Charles Lethière as a Child* by Ingres ◉ (p. 213) and an exceptional group of drawings and lithographs by Jean Dubuffet.

'Purgatory'
Auguste Rodin
Pen, brown ink, brown wash, white gouache
France, c.1890

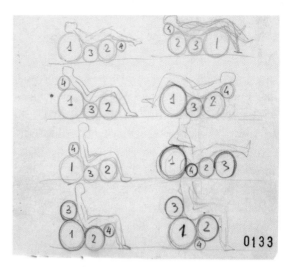

Sketch for 'Tube Chair'
Joe Colombo
Drawing on paper
Italy, 1969

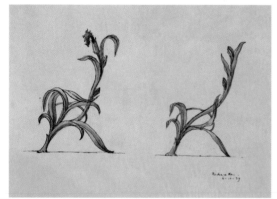

'Two chairs for a fairytale'
Emilio Terry
Drawing
France, 20th century

'Tissu Simultané' fabric design no. 30
Sonia Delaunay
Watercolour on white paper
France, 1924

Wallpaper

Thanks to the designer Victor Poterlet and the wallpaper manufacturer Jacques Turquetil, wallpaper was included in the Musée des Arts Décoratifs from the very beginning. In 1882, an exhibition of wallpaper prompted donations from manufacturers. Other gifts and purchased followed.

In 1967, the major *Three Centuries of Wallpaper* exhibition was organised to celebrate the creation of the Wallpaper Department. In 1982, the purchase of some 800 wallpapers at the auction of the collections of the manufacturers Réveillon and Jacquemart & Bénard, and the acquisition of the collection of the Leroy-Desfossé & Karth factory, considerably enlarged the museum's collection from 4,000 to over 300,000 pieces. One of the earliest wallpapers is a 17th-century 'dominoed' paper ◉ with a fleur-de-lis motif. But there are considerably more works dating from 1780 onwards. With its pilasters and rose garlands framing scenes from Greek mythology, the wallpaper printed by the Arthur & Grenard manufactory around that time is a fine example of the decorative richness and refinement which printing techniques could then achieve. The contemporary panels of arabesques by the Réveillon manufactory evoke the boudoirs of Marie-Antoinette's time.

The spectacular scenic wallpapers produced in the first half of the 19th century depict idyllic landscapes, historical scenes and cityscapes. *Brazil* ◉ (1862), with its marvellous birds and exuberant vegetation is a brilliant illustration of the fashion for exoticism which swept Europe at that time. Art Nouveau and Art Deco artists forsook the virtuosity and spatial illusionism of the Second Empire for flat repetitions of stylised motifs. In the 1920s and 30s papers were embossed, flocked*, gilt* or silvered in the styles then in fashion. The department had a major collection of wallpapers designed by Ruhlmann showing the extent to which this cabinetmaker sought to master every aspect of interior decoration. The modernist movement is also represented by wallpaper samples by Le Corbusier.

Apart from constant technical experiments, the contemporary period has also been marked by the increasingly frequent forays into the wallpaper field by artists. After Andy Warhol (1928–87) and Roy Lichtenstein ◉ (p. 219)

Marcoux paper wall hanging
Woodblock-printed, re-inked in three colours
17th century

'Brazil'
Scenic wallpaper
Louis-Joseph Fuchs
Jules Desfossé manufactory
Continuous paper, hand-painted ground,
woodblock-printed
Paris, 1862

Paper wall hanging
Réveillon manufactory
Vergé paper, 23-colour woodblock print
France, 1775

Wallpaper

(1923–97), designers such as Jean Vigne ● (born 1937) also explored this universe.

Computer-assisted design now enables wallpaper to be composed 'à la carte' by the client, who can now arrange his or her own selection of motifs. Reflecting this vitality, the department, has an encyclopaedic reference centre ranging from masterpieces to the most commercial products.

'Foxgloves'
Sketch for a wallpaper
Atelier Martine, designer
Desfossé & Karth, manufacturer
Gouache on Canson paper
Paris, c.1912

'Wallpaper with blue floor interior'
Roy Lichtenstein
Card, flat-frame print
Los Angeles, 1992

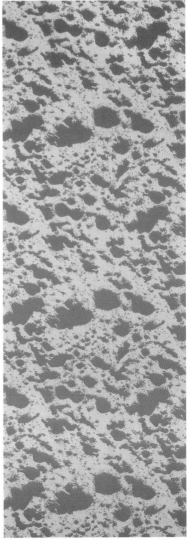

'Apollo' wallpaper
Jean Vigne
Flat-frame print
Paris, 1970

Glass

From its founding in the second half of the 19th century, the Musée des Arts Décoratifs has always attached great importance to creation in glass. Its collection, gradually enlarged over the years, now comprises over 4,000 works dating from the Middle Ages to the present day.

To do justice to this exceptional heritage—the most important glass collection in a French museum—the Centre du Verre was created in 1982, and renamed the Glass Department in 2006.

Among the department's jewels are its collection of 16th–18th-century French façon-de-Venise glass, and an exceptional collection of opaline and crystal pieces from the Restauration period. At the dawn of the 20th century, Art Nouveau is also very well represented with unique works by Rousseau, Gallé, Daum, Lalique, Henry Cros and François Décorchemont, whose archives are also in the museum. To which one should add the name of Maurice Marinot in the 1930s. Glass had become a means of formal expression and as such reflected trends in contemporary art. Recently the great names of French art and international designers, artists and artisans have worked in glass: César, Bernard Dejonghe, Eric Dietman, Ettore Sottsass, Tapio Wirkkala, Dale Chihuly, Richard Meitner, to name but a few.

With the Documentation Centre, the Glass Department manages a collection of documents including over 3,000 books, 900 ancient and modern commercial catalogues, specialised reviews and monographic studies devoted to glassmakers. This collection is regularly consulted for exhibitions and publications initiated or organised by the Glass Department or to which it contributes, such as *Contemporary French Glassmakers, Art and Industry* (1982), *Bohemian Glass 1400–1989, Masterpieces from the Czech Museums* (1989) and *Venice and Façon de Venise* (2003), among others.

The Glass Department aims to be a privileged place for exchanges and research for art lovers, artists and glass manufacturers.

Documentation Centre

The progressive enrichment of the museum's collections has gone hand in hand with the constant enlargement of its collection of documents covering various aspects of the works: historic, artistic, technical, economic, etc.

This collection was previously divided into several sections (Middle Ages-Renaissance, wallpaper, contemporary art, fashion, advertising, etc.) reflecting the institution's various departments. Since January 2001, these centres were amalgamated into a single entity, the Documentation Centre of the Arts Décoratifs' museums, a place of information on the decorative arts, fashion, textiles and advertising.

The Documentation Centre's vocation is to inform the French and foreign public, amateur and professional, artist or manufacturer, from the group of schoolchildren with their teacher to the journalist. This can be done in the museum or via Internet. Period, style, artist, use, craft, material: the works listed and documented in the databases are photographed and presented to the public according to multiple criteria. The document archives is composed of books and a thematic documentation unparalleled in France.

The systematic digitalisation of the museum's collections, in progress since 1991, now includes over 200,000 dossiers on works and thematic dossiers available to all at the Documentation Centre by appointment. Acting as an interface for passing on the knowledge of the museum's scientific staff to the general public, in collaboration with the curators, experts and international scholars, this database complements the more general information available in the Arts Décoratifs' library.

Glossary

Acanthus
plant with crenellated leaves used by the ancient Greeks to decorate the capitals of Corinthian columns. The acanthus has been a recurrent motif in architectural decoration and the decorative arts from the Middle Ages to the present day.

Alabaster
a type of gypsum quarried in England and Tuscany. This soft, white translucent stone was used in sculpture, and in the Middle Ages sometimes cut into sheets to close off small bays.

Amaranth
dark red-coloured Brazilian wood used in marquetry.

Amber
fragile fossilised resin varying in colour from pale yellow to red. Rare and expensive, it was sculpted like ivory.

Barbotine
clay mixed with water used in ceramics to stick on accessories (handles) or for making pieces such as vases and statuettes by pouring into a mould.

Baroque (pearl)
irregularly-shaped natural pearl used in jewellery from the Renaissance to Art Nouveau.

Bas-relief
sculpture whose relief hardly protrudes from the ground.

Biscuit
unglazed white porcelain.

Bronze
alloy of copper and tin. First used in the 3rd millennium BC, initially for weapons and domestic utensils then later for furniture and statuary. Appreciated for its hardness and smooth, close-knit texture, it was often patinated, gilt or silvered. The object is first cast in a mould then reworked cold (elimination of casting defects, chasing, engraving). In the 18th century, it was widely used to decorate marquetried furniture and for clocks, candelabrums, keyhole plaques, mouldings, etc. The 'lost wax' casting process consists in sculpting the object in wax then making a mould of it. When the mould is heated the wax melts and runs out and the bronze can then be cast.

Bur, burred
knotted parts of certain trees (elm, ash, maple) appreciated for their rich motifs.

Cabinet
a precious piece of furniture with drawers and compartments. A 'cabinet' can also be a room in which a collection is kept.

Cabinetmaking
originally joinery decorated with ebony veneer, then, more generally, with all precious woods. The word now means the making of all luxury furniture.

Cane
woven rush or rattan stems used for chair seats or basket weaving.

Ceramic
This word, derived from the Greek *keramos* (potter's clay), designates all objects made with clay and which, during firing at various temperatures undergo an irreversible physiochemical conversion which makes them extremely hard.

Champlevé
an enamelling technique consisting in gouging out a design in a metal plaque then placing enamel in the resulting declivities. The ungouged divisions separate the areas of coloured enamel.

Crystal
rock crystal (natural crystal) is a hard, translucent hyaline quartz found mainly in the Alps. It was used in the Middle Ages in precious metalwork, for cabochons, reliquary plaques, etc. Artificial crystal, similar in brilliance to natural crystal, is a glass composed of silica, potassium and lead oxide. It was invented in England in the 17th century and first produced in France, at Saint-Louis, in 1781.

Cross-cut
sawn perpendicularly to the grain of the wood, as opposed to along the grain.

the inlaying on a metal surface (usually steel) of motifs in other metals such as gold, silver and copper.

Ebony
heavy hardwood from the West Indies, Africa, South America and Madagascar whose colour ranges from dark brown to black. Considered rare and precious since the Middle Ages and used for veneering, ebony was linked to the emergence of cabinetmaking in the late 16th century. Macassar ebony, named after the Indonesian archipelago, is brown with black stripes.

Electrolysis
decomposition of a liquid by an electrical current. See electroplating.

Electroplating
process consisting in depositing a thin coat of metal (copper, gold, silver, nickel, etc.) on an ordinary metal surface. The metal to be deposited is dissolved in a saline solution. The electrical charge decomposes the saline solution and the metal is deposited on the negative electrode (cathode) and the rest of the molecules on the positive electrode (anode). The object to be plated is fixed to the cathode. Relief effects can be obtained by fixing a mould to the cathode.

Enamel
a vitrifiable, transparent, opaque, coloured or uncoloured substance used to coat glass, pottery, and metal objects to protect and/or decorate them. It becomes one with the object during firing.

Faience
clay pottery covered with an opaque white, copper-based glaze and fired at 1,000°C. In 'high-fired' faience, the metallic oxide-based decoration is applied to the unfired glaze. 'Low-firing', first used in the 17th century, consists in applying decoration to the fired glaze which is then fired a second time at a lower temperature. This technique enables the use of more delicate colours.

Figured
the figure of a piece of wood can be due to the cut or the innate properties of the wood. A few tropical hardwoods, rosewoods, for instance, can have quite spectacular figure.

Filigree
in precious metalwork, decoration made from soldered gold or silver wire. In glassmaking, decoration made from coloured glass thread.

Flock, flocking
decoration in light relief applied to wallpaper. The technique consists in sprinkling powdered textile fibres on paper freshly printed with glue.

Foliation
classical decorative motifs composed of intertwining foliage.

Formica
plastic laminate invented in 1912, composed of canvas coated in synthetic resin. It was used initially as electrical insulation then in utility furniture (kitchens) and later by contemporary designers.

Glossary

Gable
in Gothic architecture, a kind of triangular pediment, often openwork and crowned with an ornament.

Gilt, gilding
the application of a thin coat of gold to an object. Gilding with mercury or 'with ground gold' was practiced in ancient Rome. It consisted in covering an object with an amalgam of gold and mercury, the mercury then being eliminated by heating. 18th-century bronze founders achieved supreme mastery of this technique.

Giltwood
gilding by applying gold leaf to wood prepared with several coats of a glue and chalk-based primer. The last coat of primer, composed of fine-ground clay coloured red with iron oxide, is carefully sanded. The gold leaf applied to it is then polished with an agate stone.

Glass
hard, breakable, transparent material created by the fusion at around 1,000°C of a mixture of siliceous sand and potassium or sodium. The first artistic glassware appeared in the Middle East and Egypt during the third millennium BC. Sand was mixed with vegetable ashes riches in sodium. The first vessels were fashioned around a terracotta core. The technique of blowing glass began in the 1st century BC. From the 15th to the 17th century, Venice dominated European production with *cristallo*, a glass rendered perfectly transparent by the elimination of all traces of potash. In Germany in the 17th century, a more resistant, easier to engrave, potassium and chalk-based glass was developed. Acid-engraving was discovered. Bohemia supplanted Venice as the major production centre. In the 19th century, major technologic developments contributed to the development of the glass industry.

Greek fret
an ancient Greek ornamental pattern composed of a repetitive series of horizontal and vertical lines doubling back on themselves at right angles.

Grisaille
monochrome painting or decoration in white, grey and black.

Grotesque
derived from the Italian *grottesco*, in turn derived from *grotto*. A type of decoration imitating the ancient Roman frescoes unearthed in Rome in the late 15th century in the caverns beneath monuments such as the *Domus Aurea* or Titus's Baths.

Herm
Hermes, the Roman god guardian of boundaries is represented as a square block of stone surmounted by a head and/or bust without or without arms. The word also designates its interpretations in architecture and the decorative arts from the 16th century onwards.

High-relief
A sculpted relief whose figures are partially detached from the background.

Historicism
in art, a movement which emerged in the first quarter of the 19th century, whose aim was to revitalise art by imitating the art of the past.

Intarsia
different grained and coloured woods inlaid in a soft wood panel, usually poplar or lime. This technique, practiced in medieval Italy, is the ancestor of marquetry.

In-the-round
in sculpture, a figure depicted in full relief.

Ivory
a bonelike substance, usually elephant tusk, used in sculpture, marquetry and various forms of decoration.

Kingwood
a wood in the rosewood family with a contrasted grain ranging from violet to brown.

Lacquer
a viscous, toxic resin extracted by incision from Rhus verniciflua, an Asian resinous tree. It can be coloured. The technique of lacquering, invented in China, consists in applying thin coats of lacquer to an object, which are then carefully sanded in a damp atmosphere. The lacquer is then painted, sculpted, engraved or gilt.

Magot
a porcelain, ivory or hardstone figure from the Buddhist or Taoist pantheon and its European imitations.

Mahogany
red-brown hardwood with light and dark striated veins, appreciated not only for its colour, which darkens with age, but also for its beautiful polish. The most sought-after varieties come from Santo Domingo and Cuba.

Marquetry
an assemblage of pieces of wood sawn into thin sheets and glued to a piece of furniture. Marquetry is usually composed of precious woods but can include materials such as tortoiseshell, mother-of-pearl, ivory and metal.

Martin (varnish)
a technique imitating Chinese or Japanese lacquer using a copal-based varnish. Named after a famous family of 18th-century varnishers, who, although they did not invent the technique, made it their speciality.

Mother-of-pearl
a hard, white, iridescent substance grown on the inside of numerous molluscs, mainly pearl oysters, and used in luxury goods and marquetry. It can be engraved and tinted.

Palmwood
the palm tree is not a tree but a monocotyledonous plant growing in Asia and Africa. The trunk, cut into thin sheets, was used for veneering by Art Deco cabinetmakers.

Paste (glass) (pâte de verre)
glass, broken or crushed and sometimes mixed with a binder then fired at 800°C in a mould. First used by the Phoenicians and Egyptians, this technique was revived in the 19th century by Henry Cros.

Patina
the natural or artificial aging of certain objects. The natural patination of metals by oxidation can be accelerated using acid solutions (green-patinated bronze, for instance).

Perspective
the art of representing the appearance of three-dimensional objects in space on a one-dimensional plane. Invented in Florence by the architect Filippo Brunelleschi and theorised by another architect, Leon Battista Alberti, in 1435, scientific perspective prompted a veritable revolution in the visual arts.

Philactery
a small sheet of parchment inscribed with passages from the sacred texts, which the Jews attached to their arms or forehead. In medieval art, a banner bearing an inscription.

Pinnacle
in Gothic architecture, the crown of a buttress or vertical support, shaped like an edifice with a sharply pointed roof. It was adopted as a decorative motif by joiners and precious metalsmiths in the late Middle Ages.

Plastic
synthetic organic materials composed of resins of animal (milk), vegetable or mineral (petrol) origin, which harden when mixed with an additive. Mineral and vegetable components (talcum, silica, fibreglass, natural fibres)

Glossary

can increase their natural resistance. There are three main types of plastics: thermoplastics (which can be shaped when hot), thermal-hardening (their form cannot be altered once they have hardened), and elastomers (elastics).

Plywood
made by sticking thin sheets of wood together so that the fibres of one sheet are perpendicular to those of the next. Plywood is stable, light and resistant and can be bent and moulded.

Polyptych
in medieval art, a picture composed of several painted and/or sculpted panels, either fixed or movable.

Polyurethane
a urethane polymer discovered in 1937 and used mainly in foam form in furniture (chair seats) since the 1960s.

Porcelain (hard-paste)
invented by the Chinese, porcelain is a white, translucent, kaolin-based, very fine-paste ceramic. Chinese porcelain was introduced into Europe in the 15th century and imitated in the 16th century in Florence and in France in the following century. As kaolin deposits had not yet been discovered in Europe, it was replaced by a 'frit', a silica-based vitrifiable mixture. The first European hard-paste porcelain was made in Meissen in the early 18th century.

Predella
the long rectangular lower register of an altarpiece.

Psyché
A large pivotable mirror.

PVC
polyvinyl chloride, discovered in 1872, is a plastic that can be either rigid, flexible and shiny. It is used in furniture and floor and wall coverings, etc.

Quatrefoil
in architecture, an ornament with four semi-circular lobes. In sculpture, an ornament composed of four stylised leaves.

Rosewood
a dark red, often marbled Brazilian wood, used in marquetry, varying in colour from pinkish yellow to pale red, with darker grain.

Satine wood
a heavy, red, fine-grained Guinean hardwood with blond veins and shimmering reflections.

Scabelle
in the Middle Ages, a small wood stool, sometimes with a back.

Shagreen
stingray or sharkskin, prepared and tinted and used from the 18th century in luxury goods.

Stained glass
coloured glass assembled in a decorative composition mounted in lead. The earliest well-preserved stained glass windows are in Augsburg athedral (c.1100). The motif's components were cut out of panes of coloured glass with a red-hot iron or diamond. They were then painted in grisaille with vitrifiable paint and fired. In the 16th century, painted enamel was used instead of tinted glass.

Stamp
a joiner's or cabinetmaker's mark stamped or branded on a piece of furniture.

Stoneware
a very hard, entirely vitrified, impermeable opaque ceramic material fired at high temperatures.

Sycamore
a variety of maple.

Tapestry
1. A work embroidered on canvas with a needle.
2. A work woven on a loom, in which the pattern or picture is woven at the same time. The imagery is created with the coloured weft threads, which are woven through the uncoloured warp threads. Worked by pedals, the heddles separate and guide the weft threads and make a path for the shuttle. In low-warp looms, the heddle is horizontal, in high-warp looms it is vertical.

Terres d'Angleterre
A fine, creamy white faience imitating English glazed earthenware. The Pont-au-Choux manufactory, founded in Paris in 1740, made it its speciality.

Tin
a light grey metal used since the Middle Ages for everyday utensils. In the 1880s artists such as Jules Brateau attempted to bring it back into fashion in chased vases and ewers and small sculptures. Tin was also used in Boulle marquetry.

Photographic credits

Paris, Les Arts Décoratifs, © photo Philippe Chancel: cover, 79 br, 88-89, 106-107, 117 bl, 118-119, 143 b, 150-151, 170-171, 191 c; photo Jean-Marie Del Moral: p. 24, 68-69, 124-125, 144-145, 169 bl, 169 br, 198-199 ; photo Laurent-Sully Jaulmes: p. 10, 13 t, 13 br, 14, 16-17, 19, 21, 23 t, 23 c, 27, 28-29, 30 t, 30 br, 31 b, 35 c, 35 b, 36 t, 36 br, 39 tl, 39 c, 39 b, 40 bl, 41, 43, 44, 45, 46, 49 b, 53 b, 54 t, 55 c, 55 b, 57, 58, 59 c, 61, 65 c, 66, 67 t, 71 t, 71 bl, 73 tr, 75 cl, 75 cr, 76 t, 76 c, 77 b, 79 c, 81 tl, 81 tr, 82 t, 83, 85 t, 85 cl, 85 cr, 85 bl, 85 bc, 87 t, 87 cr, 87 br, 90, 92-93, 94, 97 tl, 99, 101 tl, 101 tr, 102, 103, 105, 108 t, 109, 111, 113 b, 114 t, 115, 117 tl, 117 br, 120, 123 t, 127, 128 c, 128 b, 129, 131, 133 c, 133 b, 134, 135 br, 137 tl, 137 tr, 137 cl, 137 cr, 138, 141, 143 t, 143 c, 146 b, 147 t, 149 tl, 149 bl, 149 br, 153, 155 tl, 155 tr, 155 c, 157 tr, 157 c, 157 b, 158, 159, 160, 163, 164 b, 165, 167 tl, 167 tr, 167 c, 167 br, 169 t, 169 c, 172, 173, 175, 176, 177, 178, 181 t, 181 b, 182, 183, 185, 187 tl, 187 tr, 187 bl, 187 br, 189 c, 191 t, 192, 193 b, 194 b, 195 t, 197 t, 197 cl, 203 cr, 203 b, 207, 208, 209, 211, 213 tl, 213 tr, 213 c, 214, 215 c, 215 b, 217 t, 217 c; photo Michel Pintado: p. 205 b ; photo Jean Tholance: p. 13 bg, 15, 23 b, 25, 30 bl, 31 t, 32, 35 t, 36 bl, 37, 39 tr, 40 br, 42, 49 t, 50-51, 53 t, 53 c, 54 b, 55 t, 59 t, 59 b, 60, 62, 65 tr, 65 tl, 65 b, 67 b, 70, 71 br, 73 tl, 73 b, 75 tl,75 tr, 75 b, 76 b, 77 t, 77 c, 79 tl, 79 tr, 79 bl, 81 b, 82 c, 82 b, 85 br, 87 tl, 87 cl, 87 l, 95 tr, 95 b, 101 c, 101 bl, 101 br, 108 b, 113 t, 113 c, 114 b, 116, 117 tr, 123 b, 128 t, 133 t, 135 t, 135 bl, 137 b, 146 t, 149 tr, 152, 155 b, 157 tl, 164 t, 167 bl, 181 c, 187 cl, 187 cr, 189 b, 193 c, 194 t, 195 bl, 195 br, 197 cr, 201, 203 t, 203 cl, 204, 205 tl, 205 tr, 213 b, 215 t, 217 br, 218, 219; fonds Albert Lévy: p. 147 c, 147 b.
© The Gallery Mourmans, photo Erik Hesmerg: p. 189 t.
© Fonds national d'art contemporain, Courtesy Édition Neotu Paris-France: p. 191 b; photo Bruno Scotti, Paris: p. 197 b, 200; photo Gérard Jonca, Paris: p. 193 t.
© Éditions Faton, photo J.-Y. et N. Dubois: p. 91.
© Adagp, Paris 2006: p. 127 br, 141 b, 143 c, 143 b, 144-145, 146 b, 147, 149 tl, 149 bl, 153, 155, 157 c, 165, 167 tl, 169 t, 170-171, 175 cr, 175 b, 181 t, 181 c, 182 b, 185 cl, 187 cl, 187 br, 191 t, 194 t, 205, 207, 211 tr, 211 c, 215 c, 219 t.
© Estate of Roy Lichtenstein New York–Adagp, Paris 2006: p. 219.
© FLC–Adagp, Paris 2006: p. 147 b.
© 2006 The Saul Steinberg Foundation–Artists Rights Society (ARS), New York–Adagp, Paris 2006: p. 181 t.

This book was photoengraved and printed in October 2006 by Amilcare Pizzi S.p.A., Cinisello Balsamo. Printed in Italy.

Registration of copyright: October 2006